TRAIL OF THE
CATWOMAN

Eaglemoss Ltd. 2015
1st Floor, Kensington Village, Avonmore Road,
W14 8TS, London, UK.
All rights reserved.

Editorial Director: Maggie Calmels
Editorial Managers: Richard Jackson, Ben Robinson
Editor: Will Potter
Book Design: Steve Scanlan
Introductions: Glenn Dakin

YOUR COLLECTION
DC Comics Graphic Novel Collection is published fortnightly.

DON'T MISS AN ISSUE: place a regular order with your
magazine retailer.

SUBSCRIBE and receive exclusive free gifts!
To subscribe: Visit our website at www.eaglemoss.com/dc-books
Call our hotline 0371 277 0112
Post the subscription form (which you will find inside issues
1, 2, 3, 4 & 5)

BACK ISSUES
To order back issues:
Order online at www.eaglemoss.com/dc-books
or call 0371 277 0112

UK distributor: COMAG Magazine Marketing

UK CUSTOMER SERVICES
Call: 0371 277 0112
Email: dc-books@eaglemoss.service.com
Write to: DC Comics Graphic Novel Collection, Database Factory,
Unit 4, Pullman Business Park, Pullman Way, Ringwood, Hampshire,
BH24 1HD

Australia
Call: (03) 9872 4000
E-mail: bissett@bissettmags.com.au
Write to: DC Comics Graphic Novel Collection, Bissett Magazine
Service Pty Limited, PO Box 3460 Nunawading, VIC 3131

South Africa
Call: (011) 265 4307
E-mail: service@jacklin.co.za
Write to: DC Comics Graphic Novel Collection, Eaglemoss Ltd,
Private Bag 18, Centurion 0046

OVERSEAS BACK ISSUES
Place your order with your local magazine retailer.

Visit our website: www.eaglemoss.com/dc-books

TRAIL OF THE CATWOMAN

ED BRUBAKER
WRITER

DARWYN COOKE, BRAD RADER
PENCILLERS

MIKE ALLRED, CAMERON STEW
RICH BURCHETT
INKERS

SEAN KONOT, WILLIE SCHUBERT
LETTERERS

MATT HOLLINGSWORTH, LEE LO
COLOURISTS

BATMAN #62
BILL FINGER
WRITER

BOB KANE
PENCILLER

CHARLES PARIS
INKER

Matt Idelson Editor – Original Series
Nachie Castro Assistant Editor – Orig
Lysa Hawkins Associate Editor – Origi
Ian Sattler Editor - Collected Edition

INTRODUCING...
TRAIL OF THE CATWOMAN

The cat was back on the streets, a locale that new writer Ed Brubaker was no stranger to. The old Catwoman, a glamorous super villain and selfish survivor was gone. She had disappeared in a flaming fireball in *Catwoman #94* (July 2001) and Brubaker wanted her to stay dead. With co-conspirator, artist Darwyn Cooke, he created a new Selina Kyle, who cared about the human flotsam and jetsam of Gotham's East End, and offered the kind of protection that only existed outside the rule of law.

To make a break from the past, the creative team took Selina out of the superhero genre, with all its fantastical trappings, and put her in the realm of the hard-boiled private eye, a landscape of sleeze and betrayal, where a trail of blood rarely led to a happy ending. This is a world that owes more to the sublime detective literature of Raymond Chandler, than the world of Batman.

The creators assembled their cast with care, giving Selina a family of sorts to interact with. This bruised collection of troubled souls included her fragile young friend Holly and old-school private eye Slam Bradley.

The first story arc, 'Anodyne' (2002), began with the serial slaying of streetwalkers, a hard-core opening that then completely wrong-footed the reader with the freakish fantasy of its climax. Darwyn Cooke's stylish, cinematic storytelling reflects his days storyboarding DC animations.

The second arc, with Brad Rader as penciller, took Selina into the world of police corruption. Hurting and in need of allies, Catwoman showed her claws in her thrilling new role as avenging angel of the streets.

DARWYN COOKE was a budding comics creator who worked as a graphic designer and art editor in Canada in the 1980s. In the early nineties, he was hired by Warner Bros. to work as storyboard artist on *Batman: the Animated Series* and *Superman: The Animated Series*. His graphic novel, BATMAN: EGO, published by DC Comics in 2000, brought him critical and fan acclaim. This led to his collaboration with Ed Brubaker on CATWOMAN in 2001 and the Golden Age/Silver Age adventure DC: THE NEW FRONTIER in 2004. Cooke's recent work includes both script and art on BEFORE WATCHMEN: MINUTEMEN.

ED BRUBAKER began his career as a cartoonist in the alternative comics scene, before writing for *Dark Horse Presents* in the early nineties. In 1995 he produced his first work for DC/Vertigo Visions, reviving the character PREZ. From 2000 he became a regular writer on BATMAN and CATWOMAN. For Wildstorm, he went on to write THE AUTHORITY and THE SLEEPER. During this time he also

BIOGRAPHIES

collaborated with writer Greg Rucka on the police force-focussed series GOTHAM CENTRAL. From 2004 he enjoyed huge success with an eight-year stint on *Captain America* for Marvel Comics, including the 'Winter Soldier' storyline, plus scripts for *Daredevil, Uncanny X-Men* and *Secret Avengers*. For Icon Comics he created *Criminal* with artist Sean Phillips, before the partnership launched the award-winning *Fatale* and *The Fade Out* for Image Comics from 2012.

BRAD RADER is a US comic book and animation artist whose work has graced *The Simpsons* and *King of the Hill*. In 1999 Rader won an Emmy for his work as a director on Todd McFarlane's *Spawn*. His comic book work includes THE BATMAN ADVENTURES, GOTHAM ADVENTURES and CATWOMAN for DC Comics and the graphic novel crime-thriller FOGTOWN for DC's Vertigo offshoot.

MIKE ALLRED first came to fame in the comics world in 1992 with his creator-owned character *Madman* for Tundra and Dark Horse Comics. He then brought his classic, clear-line drawing style to titles such as DC/Vertigo's THE SANDMAN, providing inks for Darwyn Cooke on CATWOMAN and pencils on *X-Statix, FF* and *Silver Surfer* for Marvel. iZOMBIE, his 2010 DC/Vertigo co-creation, with writer Chris Roberson, has been turned into a successful TV series.

THE STORY SO FAR...

Catwoman had faked her death to escape from her past and find a new way to live, a way she could believe in. Returning to Gotham City, she was at rock bottom and knew she needed a big score to get back on her feet. Her opportunity came in the form of Chantel, a bitter streetwalker with gangland connections. Sickened by her fate, she wanted to escape and regain her basic human dignity, even if it cost her life.

That word dignity touched Selina and sealed the deal. Chantel gave Selina the details of an express train carrying dirty mob money up to Montreal to trade for drugs. Selina put together a team to pull off the outrageous heist, including Stark, her former lover and mentor, a man who had been closer to her than she ever cared to admit.

Selina had another problem. Private Eye Slam Bradley had been tasked by the mayor and the mob to investigate the death of Selina Kyle. The dogged detective was closing in on secrets that had to stay buried. Then, the bodies started piling up. The Falcone family got wise to Chantel's treachery with inevitable results. In a compromised mission, Selina's team fell one by one, including the seemingly unbreakable Stark.

Slam Bradley, who had figured out Selina's past, decided to keep it all to himself. Selina got away with the money but made sure it was used to help build a future for the baby girl Chantel had left behind. The heart-rending mission confirmed Selina's belief that she needed a new direction, a role on the mean streets of Gotham City. More human, yet tougher than ever, Catwoman was on the prowl once more.

OLD GOTHAM, THE EAST END, FAR TOO LATE...

LOOKIN' FOR A PARTY?

YEAH, I AM, ACTUALLY...

... CAN YOU HELP ME OUT WITH THAT?

OH, I GUESS WE COULD WORK SOMETHIN' OUT...

GET IN.

UNT UH... SORRY, I DON'T DO CAR DATES WITH GUYS I DON'T KNOW.

OKAY, MY NAME'S BRIAN.

GLAD TO MEET YOU...?

I'M LISA.

CATWOMAN 1. January, 2002. Published monthly by DC Comics, 1700 Broadway, New York, NY 10019. POSTMASTER: Send address changes to CATWOMAN, DC Comics Subscriptions, P.O. Box 0528, Baldwin, NY 11510. Annual subscription rate $30.00. Canadian subscribers must add $12.00 for postage and GST. GST # is R125921072. All foreign countries must add $12.00 for postage. U.S. funds only. Copyright © 2002 DC Comics. All Rights Reserved. All characters featured in this issue, the distinctive likenesses thereof, and all related indicia are trademarks of DC Comics. The stories, characters and incidents mentioned in this magazine are entirely fictional. Printed on recyclable paper.
Printed in Canada.

DC Comics. A division of Warner Bros.–An AOL Time Warner Company

... YOU'VE GONE THROUGH SOME *AWFUL* STRUGGLES IN YOUR LIFE. ESPECIALLY IN THIS PAST YEAR...

AND IT'S *OBVIOUSLY* LEFT SOME SCARS.

HOW LONG HAS IT BEEN NOW SINCE YOU PUT ON THE OUTFIT?

THE *OUTFIT*? OH, YEAH... *THAT*.

WELL, YOUR SUBCONSCIOUS IS PROBABLY TRYING TO SORT OUT WHO YOU ARE *WITHOUT* THAT MASK.

ALMOST SIX MONTHS.

IT DOESN'T TAKE FREUD OR JUNG TO FIGURE *THAT* OUT.

NO, I GUESS IT *DOESN'T*. SO ARE YOU TRYING TO TELL ME IT'S *NOT* DRUGS, IT'S ALL IN MY HEAD?

IN A ROUNDABOUT WAY, *YES*.

YOUR BLOODWORK CAME BACK CLEAN, SELINA... SEE FOR *YOURSELF*.

YEAH, *hmmm*...

I JUST THOUGHT, WITH THIS *NOT SLEEPING* THING, THAT IT MIGHT STILL BE WORKING ITSELF OUT OF MY SYSTEM.

SORRY TO *DISAPPOINT* YOU. WHATEVER YOU WERE SUBJECTED TO IS *LONG GONE*, AS FAR AS I CAN TELL...

... UNLESS YOU WANT ME TO DO A *SPINAL TAP*?

NO THANKS... I'LL *PASS*.

SELINA, MY ADVICE, IF YOU REALLY *WANT* IT, IS TO TAKE ADVANTAGE OF THIS TIME...

Welcome home, Selina Kyle...

Is this where you belong?

But even if it's not, where else were you going to go?

As far as most of the world is concerned, Selina Kyle is dead... So it wasn't like you could just move back into your Park Row apartment.

But this place, no one knows about this place. Not anymore. Well, maybe *he* knows.

It's hard to say what he knows for sure.

But you hadn't even thought of this place in years. Amazing that it was still here, after all this time, and the changes that Gotham has been through.

But somehow you knew it would be, because you bought this place back in the early days to be a sanctuary...

A safe house for your friends... Holly, Monique, Darla... A secret home away from the street and the life.

Of course, all of them are long gone now, and who would have ever imagined it would be you who would need this sanctuary?

Not to hide, of course... but to slow down, take a look at your life, and the mess you've made of it.

You were a different person then. That Selina took care of people...

And how fitting that you'd have to come back to these streets, where it all began.

... and had been for as long as she could remember...

That had been one of the reasons for the mask, initially. To help provide.

That and the excitement... the adventure. Don't kid yourself that they weren't a big part of it, too.

But when did they take over?

When did you stop helping your sister, your friends, and just start helping yourself?

And when did you climb the social ladder and lose those friends entirely?

SO, THEN... WHO ARE YOU, SELINA KYLE?

Hardly any sleep last night, either.

Maybe what I need is some exercise.

My mind is probably just spinning in circles because I'm not in constant motion.

So, maybe if I work myself to exhaustion, that'll do the trick.

TWAP!

THE GOTHAM GAZETTE

SECOND BODY FOUND IN ONE WEEK

POLICE HAVE NO COMMENT ON MURDER

Anything to just shut my brain off for a few hours.

And if pushing my muscles until they tear doesn't do it...

... maybe, this sunset will...

There's nothing quite like the universe to make your problems feel small...

... if only for a moment or two.

Of course, when night falls there's always something to help you lose perspective...

RATATATTA ATT

SKREECH

Him. Of course.

BAM

BRATA TATTA TAT TAT

Gotham's own guardian angel.

In his black and white world...

KRASH

BOOM

... with his brightly-colored adversaries.

WHEN IS IT *TIME*... TO ACT LIKE A *BANANA*...?

Without him, I wouldn't have become who I am.

And I owe him so much...

ALL OF YOU! JUST *STAY* CALM!

NOBODY PANIC, JUST MOVE *ONE* STEP AT A *TIME!*

But we've been at odds from the start. Because-- No!

NO!

At odds from the start...

... Because my world is all just shades of grey, Batman.

That's why you'll never really understand me.

It's about good people being forced into bad situations.

That's my territory...

In between right and wrong.

Which is a place you can never go. And we both know it.

Just like I know I'll finally sleep tonight.

mmrrowrr?
mrrrowr?

mrrrowr?

WHAT DO YOU WANT, *Hmmm?* DIDN'T I PUT OUT ENOUGH *FOOD,* LITTLE FLUFFY GUY?

THEN GO *EAT,* OKAY? I'VE GOT SOME STUFF TO *DO* HERE!

mrrroarrr! mrrrrr!

Dr. Thompkins... Leslie... was right. The mask is part of who I am now.

But it's also part of the problem, too...

... because it became a person all on its own.

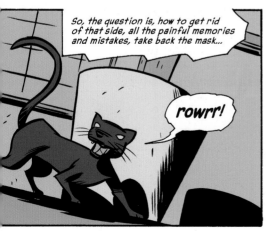

So, the question is, how to get rid of that side, all the painful memories and mistakes, take back the mask...

rowrr!

... and still be able to sleep at night. Still be able to live with myself.

I'm not sure if I can do all that, really...

... but I think I know how to try...

SURPLU

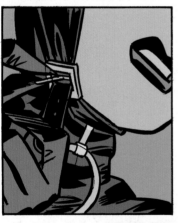

We can skip the tail for now...

And figure out what else to skip as time goes on.

It feels good to be a part of it all again.

The city lights...

The night...

Maybe it feels right again, for the first time in a long time.

SO, WAS THAT *YOU* THE OTHER DAY?

COULDN'T LET HIM *SHOOT* YOU, COULD I?

I'D HAVE SURVIVED IT.

YOU'RE WELCOME.

WHAT IS *THIS*, EXACTLY? THE *NEW YOU*?

I'M NOT *SURE* YET. WHAT DO YOU *THINK*?

IT LOOKS... *PRACTICAL.*

THAT'S WHAT *I* THOUGHT, TOO.

SO, DID YOU GO TO SEE DR. THOMPKINS?

YEAH, A FEW TIMES, ACTUALLY... YOU TOLD HER WHO I *WAS*?

I TRUST HER IMPLICITLY. YOUR SECRET'S *SAFE* WITH HER.

I'M *NOT* MAD.

IT'S KIND OF *NICE*, HAVING SOMEONE KNOW I'M STILL AROUND...

Maybe this will actually work. I'll have to give it time.

But the mask felt good again... It felt like me.

Whoever *that* is --

CHK CHK CHK

CHK CHK -- WHAT THE HELL? CHK

SOMEONE TRYING TO PICK MY LOCK?

CHK

AHH! WAIT!

OH... MY... GOD...

HOLLY?

SELINA? WHAT ARE *YOU* DOING HERE? I *THOUGHT*--?

YOU'RE *BACK* ON THE *STREETS?* OH, HOLLY...

DON'T *LOOK* AT ME LIKE THAT, SELINA.

YOU DON'T *UNDERSTAND*...

SO *MAKE* ME.

THIS'S JUST *SO* WEIRD... I JUST REMEMBERED WHERE I HID THESE *KEYS*, BECAUSE I NEEDED SOMEPLACE *SAFE* TO CRASH.

BUT I *NEVER* THOUGHT I'D RUN INTO *YOU!* WE ALL THOUGHT--

WAIT-- WHAT DO YOU MEAN BY *SAFE?*

WHAT'S *WRONG?*

BUT, IF YOU'RE *BACK*...

... YOU *MUST KNOW,* SELINA...

... SOMEONE'S *KILLING US* OUT THERE.

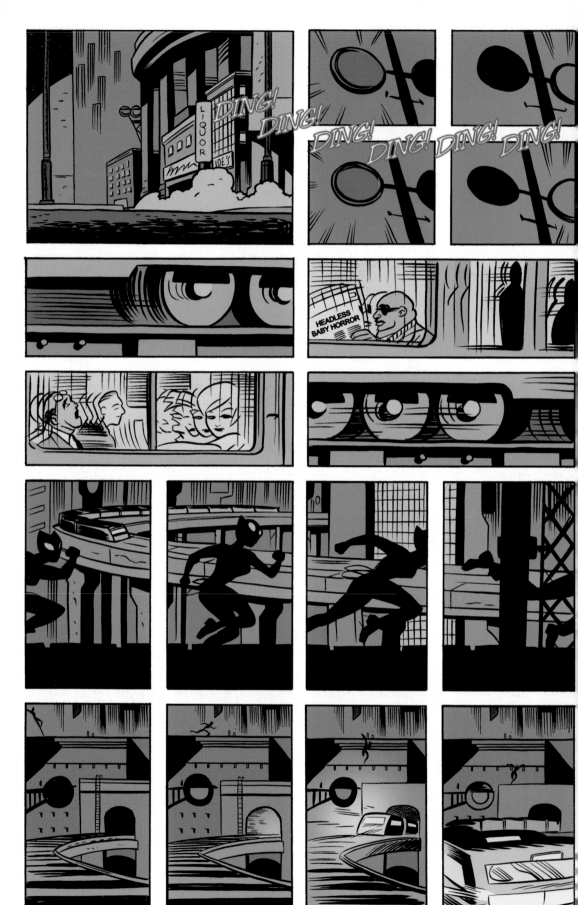

Looks like they've beefed up the security since my last visit...

CHANK

Not that they'll stop me, but it does make it more complicated.

POOM

WHAT THE HELL--?!

FIRE!

DEEOOO DEEOOO DEEOO

OO DE

SKANG

SKANG

SKANG

POP!

They're probably searching the whole complex by now, but it should be safe down here.

SNIK

Not like there's anything of real value in the morgue...

But it does have what I'm looking for--

Jane Doe 4

Information.

Jane D
Jane Doe #2
Jane Doe #3
Jane Doe #4

TEC

uspected cause o
as usual, there were tr
are signs of suffocation an
this case. The bones were
l organs appear to have
uperized as victi

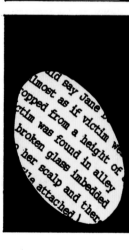

d say Jane D
almost as if victim w
opped from a height of
ictim was found in alley
broken glass imbedded
her scalp and ther
le attached

Damn it--
It's just
like Holly
said...

IT'S BEEN GOING ON FOR WEEKS, SELINA...

... BODIES ARE JUST *TURNING UP* IN ALLEYS, ALL BEATEN AND *BLOODY.*

MOST OF THE GIRLS I KNOW ARE SCARED TO DEATH.

ARE THE POLICE PUTTING *ANY MORE* MANPOWER ON THE STREETS?

HA! RIGHT. THEY COULDN'T CARE *LESS!* YOU KNOW HOW IT IS... WE'RE NOT *REAL CITIZENS* TO THEM.

YEAH...

... I GUESS I *DO* KNOW HOW THAT IS.

NICE TO SEE THAT NO MATTER *HOW MUCH* GOTHAM CHANGES, SOME THINGS STILL STAY THE SAME...

... LIKE HOW MOST OF THIS CITY WOULD LOVE FOR THE WHOLE EAST END TO JUST FALL INTO THE ATLANTIC.

SO, YOU WANT TO TELL ME WHY YOU LEFT THE *CONVENT?* AND WHY YOU'RE BACK WORKING ON THE *STREETS?*

OH, *C'MON,* SELINA. IT'S NOT LIKE *THAT...* IT'S JUST...

... THAT PLACE WASN'T *RIGHT* FOR ME, OKAY? I COULDN'T *HANDLE* IT.

AND I SURE AS HELL WASN'T GONNA BECOME A *NUN!*

IT WAS GOOD ENOUGH FOR *MAGGIE.*

NO... IT *WASN'T.*

MAGGIE LEFT *WITH ME.*

WHAT?! WHEN DID *THIS* HAPPEN?

A *LONG* TIME AGO, SELINA... WE WENT OUT TO THE WEST COAST. BUT I LOST TRACK OF HER A COUPLE OF YEARS AGO AFTER SHE FELL IN LOVE WITH SOME GUY...

... THEN I DRIFTED BACK TO GOTHAM LAST YEAR.

I DON'T *GET IT...* I THOUGHT MAGGIE'D FOUND HER PEACE IN LIFE?

I THINK SHE HAD A *CRISIS OF FAITH,* SELINA... IT HAPPENS.

I *KNOW.* BELIEVE ME... I JUST THOUGHT... *DAMN...*

WHY DIDN'T EITHER OF YOU TRY TO *CONTACT* ME?

FOR THE LAST FEW YEARS, WE THOUGHT YOU WERE *DEAD.*

Umm... WELL...

Oh... YEAH.

WELL, YOU CAN'T BELIEVE EVERYTHING YOU READ.

NO, APPARENTLY NOT.

SO, WHAT HAPPENS NOW, SELINA?

NOW?

WELL, *FIRST* WE'RE *BOTH* GOING TO GET SOME MUCH NEEDED SLEEP...

... AND THEN TONIGHT...

... I'M GOING TO GO OUT AND TRY TO STEAL US SOME *ANSWERS.*

Guess they won't mind if I borrow their copier...

I'd rather not just take this report, on the off-chance the cops decide to get off their butts and actually do something.

WHIRR-CHK-BEEP

WHAT THE HELL IS *THIS?*

CLASSIFIED INFORMATION, I'M AFRAID.

This really isn't a good start to your new life, Selina...

THUMP!

Making amateur mistakes and assaulting cops.

So, where do I go from here?

Solving crimes hasn't exactly been what I'm famous for.

But still, with all my experience on the other side of the law...

... Maybe I can see things that the police would never notice.

EEERRK

Sometimes a different point of view is enough.

But that isn't the real problem.

The real problem is the police aren't looking that hard for clues in the first place.

For the exact reason Holly said...

These murder victims don't qualify as people to them.

And as long as the killer isn't bragging to the media, their deaths are acceptable.

Their pain is the price of doing business.

Like paying taxes.

So who speaks for them, then?

If not the police?

Batman?

No. While he may care, these women aren't that high on his list, either.

As far as he's concerned, they've chosen a life of crime, and while victims, they are far from innocent.

But I've felt the fear they feel, and the pain.

The pain of that lost innocence.

And once you've lost that, it's so much easier for them to just take everything else, too.

ROWRR!

Damn.

Too late.

WHAT THE HELL IS GOING ON...?

Does this guy somehow think he'll be less conspicuous running down the street naked instead of in blood-stained clothes?

Oh, I see...

So much for running down the street. But that still doesn't explain him stripping.

Maybe that's just his thing...

In any case, let's see what he left behind...

No money, no I.D.... Just this...

DAVE'S ALL NITER

WHHEEEEEOOOOOOOOOO

Damn.

OVER HERE!

BAR

WHHEEEEEOOOOOOOOO

WHEEOOO

NO... NO, I *DIDN'T* GET A GOOD LOOK.

HIS FACE WAS ALL COVERED IN *BLOOD.* I COULD ONLY SEE HIS *EYES,* PEERIN' *OUT* AT ME...

... THOSE *EYES...*

OKAY, BURTON... I NEED YOU TO CORDON OFF THIS AREA.

AND FISCHER--

FISCHER?! WHAT THE *HELL* DO YOU THINK YOU'RE *DOING?*

AW, *C'MON,* SARGE...

SHE'S *JUST* A HOOER...

YEAH, I KNOW. AND *PROTOCOL* SAYS THE OFFICER IN *CHARGE* ROLLS THE STIFF.

NOW *GIMME* THAT, YOU STUPID ROOKIE!

ROTTEN PIGS...

FREEZE!

They walk in her blood to take her last ten dollars, because they think she's not a person. But they're wrong...

She was. They all were...

WHO *SAID* THAT?!

And I will speak for them. Because no one else will.

el GATO

NO, IT'S GOING TO BE *ALL RIGHT*... JUST *RELAX*.

AM I GONNA *DIE*, DOCTOR THOMPKINS?

OF *COURSE* NOT...

TAP

'CAUSE I DON'T *FEEL SO GOOD*... I THINK I SHOT MYSELF...

DANNY SAID IT WASN'T LOADED, THOUGH...

TAP TAP TAP

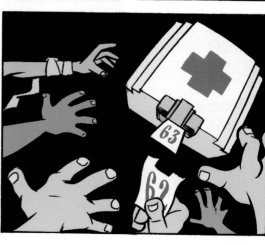

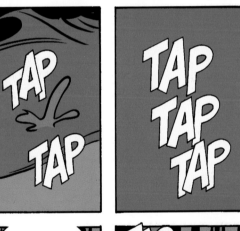

Uh, *YES...* I HAVE.

HOW CAN I *HELP?*

WELL, THERE'S SOME- ONE THE BATMAN USES WHEN HE NEEDS INFORMATION...

A WOMAN CALLED *ORACLE...*

BUT I DON'T *EXACTLY* HAVE HER PHONE NUMBER...

... AND I *NEED* SOME INFORMATION, FAST.

I HAVE THAT NUMBER, SELINA.

I COULD CALL *FOR* YOU, IF THAT'S WHAT YOU'RE ASKING.

IF SHE KNOWS IT'S FOR *ME,* SHE *MAY NOT* WANT TO--

I'LL *MAKE* HER UNDERSTAND, DON'T WORRY.

I NEED WHATEVER SHE CAN GET ABOUT THIS CAR, I WROTE DOWN THE LICENSE AND MAKE AND MODEL.

THANK YOU, REALLY...

I'LL CALL YOU AS SOON AS I HAVE ANYTHING.

I'M SORRY I HAD TO WAKE YOU UP.

IT'S ALL RIGHT... I APPRECIATE THAT YOU *KNOCKED* INSTEAD OF JUST *BREAKING IN.*

I LIKE THE *NEW LOOK*, BY THE WAY... IS IT HELPING YOUR *SLEEP* ANY?

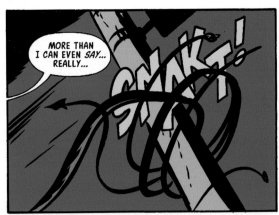

MORE THAN I CAN EVEN *SAY*... REALLY...

And it's true... The last few nights, since I've been going out like this...

... I've been sleeping like a baby.

I haven't felt this good since the first few months I was wearing the mask.

And maybe it has as much to do with having some idea of a mission, as it does with the mask.

THE EAST END...

HOW MUCH LONGER'RE YOU GUYS GONNA BE? IT'S AFTER FOUR A.M....

WE'LL BE *DONE* WHEN WE'RE *DONE*, OFFICER... THIS IS A CRIME SCENE INVESTIGATION, NOT A TRACK MEET.

WHAT THE HELL...?

MAYBE IF YOU BOYS IN BLUE'D DO A LITTLE LESS WALKING ALL OVER POTENTIAL EVIDENCE, WE COULD GET OUT OF HERE A BIT SOONER...

YEAH, *WHATEVER*...

HEY, JERRY... COME LOOK AT *THIS*.

WHATTAYA GOT?

I'M NOT SURE IT'S ANYTHING, BUT IT'S *WEIRD*...

... TAKE *YOUR TIME*.

YEAH, WEIRD... BUT MAYBE THIS MUD WAS SOFT EARLIER OR SOMETHING.

OR IT WAS A *REALLY* FAT CAT.

NAH, IT HASN'T RAINED IN *WEEKS*, AND THIS IS *HARD* PACKED...

...SEE? I HARDLY MADE A DENT.

WHAK

OKAY, SO MAYBE IT WAS A REALLY *REALLY* FAT CAT. IT'S *WEIRD*, I AGREE, BUT I DON'T THINK IT PERTAINS TO *THIS* INVESTIGATION, CHRIS...

... I'M AFRAID THE *ONLY* EVIDENCE WE'RE GONNA FIND THAT'S *USEFUL* IS THE LICENSE PLATE ON HIS CAR. AT LEAST WE CAN TRACK THAT DOWN.

UNLESS YOU THINK THESE HOOKERS ARE ALL GETTING KILLED BY A *CAT*?

KL'K

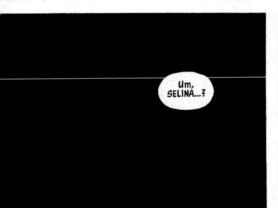

Um, SELINA...?

THERE'S, uh... SOMEONE'S ON THE PHONE FOR YOU.

THEY HAVE A NAME?

LESLIE SOMEONE...

I FORGET, THOMPSON?

Honest *Jay Little*
USED CARS

EXCUSE ME, MA'AM...

IS THERE ANYTHING *SPECIFIC* YOU'RE LOOKING FOR?

BECAUSE YOU *SEEM* LIKE THE KIND OF WOMAN WHO'D FIT *PERFECTLY* BEHIND THE WHEEL OF THAT CLASSIC *PORSCHE* CONVERTIBLE YOU'RE LOOKING AT.

I WAS THINKING THE *SAME THING*, REALLY... ARE *YOU* HONEST JAY LITTLE?

THAT'S *ME*, JUST LIKE ON THE SIGN... WHY DO YOU *ASK?*

WELL, I FIGURED IF YOU WERE THE *OWNER*, WE MIGHT BE ABLE TO GO SOME PLACE *PRIVATE* TO... *NEGOTIATE* THE PRICE.

IT'S A LITTLE OUT OF MY RANGE.

A-- A BUSINESSMAN IS *ALWAYS* WILLING TO NEGOTIATE... JUST COME INTO MY OFFICE AND WE CAN GET MORE *COMFORTABLE.*

THAT'S *JUST* WHAT I HAD IN MIND.

OFFICE

Hunh-- GUESS I LEFT MY BLINDS CLOSED...

JUST ONE LESS THING TO WORRY ABOUT THOUGH, *RIGHT*, HONEY?

I'M ASKING THE QUESTIONS, HONEST JAY...

WHO WAS THE BUYER?

I DON'T *KNOW*-- HE JUST HAD A CHECK CASHING I.D., BUT IT DIDN'T REALLY *LOOK* LIKE HIM.

WHAT *DID* HE LOOK LIKE, THEN?

SERIOUSLY? HE LOOKED A HELLUVA LOT LIKE *TODD RUSSELL*, THE ACTOR.

I KID YOU NOT...

I DIDN'T TELL THE *COPS* THAT, THOUGH-- OR ABOUT HIS I.D. BEIN' FAKE.

ARE YOU TRYING TO TELL ME A *FAMOUS ACTOR* IS MURDERING THESE WOMEN?

NAW. IT WASN'T *HIM*... HE JUST *LOOKED LIKE* HIM. THE VOICE WAS ALL WRONG.

SO... uh... YOU'RE NOT GONNA BLOW THE WHISTLE TO THE *HEAT*, ARE YOU? I'M JUST TRYIN' TO MAKE A *LIVING*, Y'KNOW?

I GOT A WIFE AND KIDS.

I'M NOT INTERESTED IN HOW YOU CHEAT THE *I.R.S.*, HONEST JAY...

BUT YOUR LACK OF RESPECT FOR YOUR *WIFE*...

NOW, *THAT'S* A DIFFERENT STORY ALTOGETHER.

OKAY-- I NEED YOU TO GET OUT THERE AND TELL EVERYONE YOU KNOW NOT TO TAKE ANY DATES WITH GUYS WHO LOOK LIKE MOVIE STARS...

WHAT'RE YOU GOING TO DO?

WELL, I'VE GOT *ONE* MORE LEAD TO CHASE DOWN TONIGHT, BUT IT MEANS A LITTLE UNDERCOVER WORK...

DO YOU-- DO YOU THINK WE REALLY SHOULD'VE JUST *LEFT HIM* LIKE THAT?

OH, C'MON HOLLY-- DON'T TELL ME YOU'VE *COMPLETELY* LOST YOUR SENSE OF *HUMOR.*

NO, I JUST DON'T WANT TO GET ANYONE IN ANY *TROUBLE,* THAT'S ALL...

YOU KNOW AS WELL AS I DO, THERE'S *NO AVOIDING* TROUBLE...

MOVIE NEWS WEEKLY

INSIDE THE LIFE OF TODD RUSSELL

Which is what I'm telling myself around nine that night as I nurse a drink in the diviest bar in the East End...

... dangling myself as bait for a killer.

Which is possibly not the brightest idea I've ever had.

DAVE'S ALL NIGHTER

THIS SEAT TAKEN?

HELP YOURSELF.

SO, uh... I HAVEN'T SEEN YOU IN HERE BEFORE, HAVE I?

I DON'T KNOW, MAYBE.

OH, WELL... I'VE GOT THIS *PLACE* NEAR HERE, IT'S KIND OF AN OLD FACTORY BUILDING, BUT I'VE GOT A LITTLE *APARTMENT* IN IT... SORT OF...

AND...?

I JUST THOUGHT, MAYBE IF YOU WERE TRYING TO FIND A *PARTY*...

WHAT KIND OF PARTY IS *THAT*? JUST THE *TWO* OF US?

I DON'T KNOW, FROM WHERE *I'M* SITTING, IT LOOKS LIKE IT'D BE A PRETTY *GREAT* PARTY THAT WAY.

MY-- AREN'T WE *FORWARD*?

I'M SORRY, MAYBE I GOT THE *WRONG* IDEA... ARE YOU *WAITING* FOR SOMEONE?

KIND OF...

A GUY WHO LOOKS A LITTLE LIKE *TODD RUSSELL*. I MET HIM IN HERE ONCE...

HUNH-- DOESN'T SOUND *FAMILIAR*...

WOULD YOU EXCUSE ME FOR A MINUTE, I NEED TO USE THE HEAD...

Great, Selina... maybe if you're lucky you'll be batting off flies all night.

BIGANTE

Good to know my disguise is working, I guess, and at least that guy was sort of cute. Now if my movie star look-alike would just show up.

BIGANTE

That's some long bathroom break, guess I scared him...

BIG

WAIT A *SECOND*...

BIGANTE

BIGANTE

HEY! THAT'S THE *MEN'S*--

CRACK!

Damn it...

DAMN IT.

Of course, it's Gotham, so of course he's got to be a freak...

Damn it.

HEY, ARE YOU OKAY?

MEN

SO, YOU LIKE, *LIVE* HERE?

YEAH-- THE RENT'S CHEAP...

HA HA HA!

Damn it. I had him right in front of me and I was too blind to see it.

ACTUALLY, MY FAMILY OWNS THIS BUILDING. SO I USE THIS AS AN *APARTMENT* WHEN I'M IN THE CITY...

What did he say? He lives in an old factory building...?

There are at least a few of those in the East End.

Y'KNOW... I USUALLY DON'T GO TO PLACES, LIKE *APARTMENTS* AND STUFF, WITH NEW GUYS...

"... IT'S JUST NOT *SAFE* THESE DAYS."

BUT YOU SEEM LIKE SUCH A *NICE* GUY, TODD...

I LIKE TO THINK SO...

Sometimes you just get lucky... Not usually, but sometimes.

Of course, I've always thought I had better luck than most people, certainly...

... But tonight, on the trail of a killer...

By the skin of my teeth...

EEII!AAA!

... I literally arrived in the nick of time.

And if that's not luck, I don't know what is.

Yet right now he seems more terrified of me than anyone has ever been.

... YOU DON'T UNDERSTAND...

I SWEAR...

Something about this just isn't right...

MAYBE YOU'D *BETTER* EXPLAIN THIS ALL TO ME, AFTER ALL...

NOT JUST NOW, NO.

WHAT? YOU-- YOU'RE NOT GONNA *HURT* ME...?

YOU WERE THERE THE *OTHER NIGHT*-- IN THE *ALLEY*...

I HAD TO *CHANGE* TO GET AWAY...

BARELY MADE IT...

CHANGE?

MY GOD... THE CAT.

CHEWING GUM

"MY FACE DIDN'T LOOK RIGHT... I WASN'T SUPPOSED TO BE *UGLY*..."

"SO I *FIXED* IT."

YOU COULD JUST *DO* THAT? HOW DID YOU KNOW?

I *DIDN'T KNOW*... I JUST *WISHED* IT, I GUESS...

WHAT ABOUT *BEFORE* THAT DAY, DO YOU REMEMBER ANYTHING *AT ALL* BEFORE THEN?

JUST LITTLE *FLASHES*...

"A *WAR* OR SOMETHING...

LIAR!

Well, that went well, Selina... Let's not forget the whole "psycho" aspect of our psycho killer.

STAND STILL!

STOP *RUNNING,* DAMN YOU!

SKLURCH!

Oh, yeah... That was effective...

NO!

UNNHH!

SKASH

NO MORE RUNNING!

NO MORE ANYTHING!

WHOMP!

Don't know if this'll work...

SNIK

... But I have to try something.

Oh my god...
I can't beat him.

Have to get away.

I have to get away. This is too big for me...

I *SAID*, NO MORE *RUNNING!*

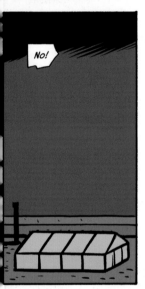

No!

Damn it!

CRA*SH!*

YOU REALLY SHOULDN'T'VE *LIED* TO ME...

Oh....

The hell with it...

ZZZZZT!

THAT... HURT...

.... BUT YOU *STILL* DON'T GET IT, DO YOU?

OH...

I WOULDN'T SAY *THAT*...

WHAT'VE YOU *DONE?*

Y'KNOW, I'M NOT REALLY *SURE...*

OH, *GROSS.*

WAIT, WHAT'RE YOU *DOING?*

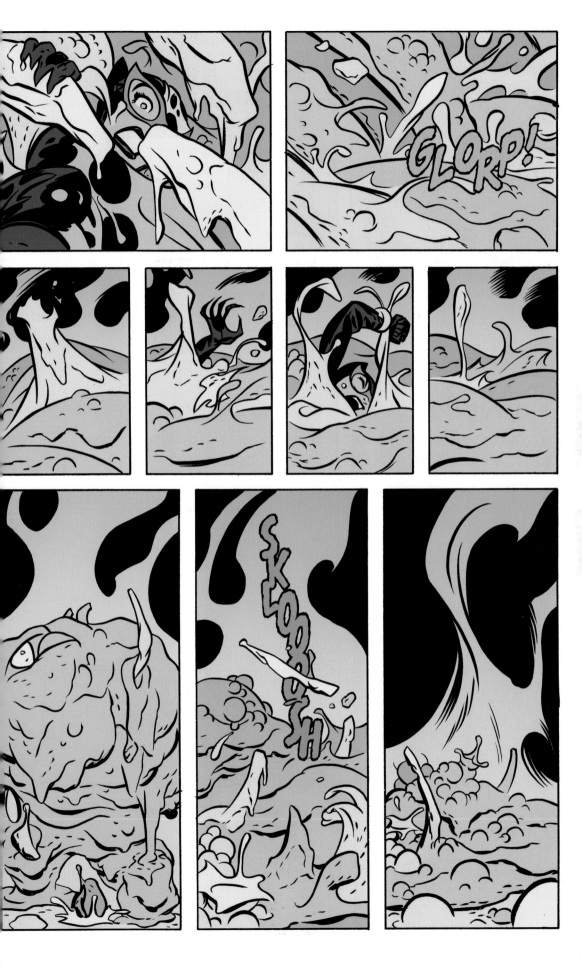

I DON'T *CARE*, SELINA...

... YOU'RE *NOT* TO USE THE SIGNAL AGAIN, UNDERSTAND? THAT'S FOR THE *POLICE*.

I DIDN'T KNOW HOW *ELSE* TO GET HOLD OF YOU. YOU SHOULD REALLY GET A *BEEPER* OR SOMETHING...

I DON'T THINK SO.

IN HERE?

YEAH, BUT... uh... BE *CAREFUL*.

CHANK!

PLEASE... HELP ME...

... HELP ME...

SO *THEN* WHAT HAPPENED, SELINA?

I DON'T KNOW... I GUESS HE TOOK IT WHEREVER HE *TAKES* THINGS LIKE THAT.

ARKHAM ASYLUM OR *S.T.A.R. LABS.* SOMEPLACE.

NATIONAL

MAN, I CAN'T *BELIEVE* IT... YOU USED THE *SIGNAL.* THAT IS *SO* COOL.

YEAH, IT *WAS* KIND OF COOL...

SO *ANYWAY,* I'VE BEEN *THINKING,* HOLLY...

... I'M NOT SURE EXACTLY WHERE I'M *GOING* WITH THIS WHOLE *HELPING PEOPLE* THING... BUT ONE THING I DO KNOW...

... I DON'T WANT *YOU* OR ANYONE ELSE I CARE ABOUT WORKING ON THE STREET.

SO, I WANT TO *HIRE YOU.*

HIRE *ME?* TO DO WHAT?

WELL, IF I'M GOING TO TRY TO DO THIS *RIGHT,* I NEED SOMEONE WHO BLENDS IN WITH THE STREET LIFE A LITTLE BETTER THAN I DO ANYMORE...

... SO, I WANT *YOU* TO BE MY EYES AND EARS.

IT'S A HIGH-PAYING GIG, BY THE WAY.

I'VE STASHED AWAY A LOT OVER THE YEARS, ENOUGH TO LIVE ON *COMFORTABLY* FOR THE REST OF OUR LIVES. AND IF THAT RUNS OUT...

... WELL, I CAN ALWAYS GET *MORE*, CAN'T I?

SO... WHAT DO YOU SAY?

I SAY, WHEN DO I *START*?

YOU ALREADY *DID*... IT WAS YOU WHO BROUGHT THESE MURDERS TO MY ATTENTION IN THE FIRST PLACE...

SO JUST KEEP DOING WHAT YOU DID.

OKAY, SO THEN, WHAT DO WE DO *NOW*?

WELL, TONIGHT I'LL BE GOING OUT AGAIN, BUT RIGHT NOW I'VE GOT TO GO SEE A *FRIEND*...

... SOMEONE I OWE A *LOT* TO.

SELINA, I *CAN'T* ACCEPT THIS...

LESLIE, I *INSIST*... IT'S JUST TO HELP YOU RUN THINGS A LITTLE.

IT'S *REALLY* NOT MUCH, YOU DESERVE A LOT MORE.

IT'S JUST-- WELL...

I *PROMISE* YOU, THE PEOPLE WHO *LOST* IT DESERVED A *LOT* WORSE... AND I'M SURE THEY NEVER MISSED IT, EITHER.

OH, VERY WELL... BUT YOU REALLY DON'T HAVE TO DO THIS. I GET QUITE A FEW *GRANTS* TO RUN THIS PLACE, REALLY.

I KNOW, BUT I JUST WANT TO GIVE SOMETHING *BACK* TO YOU. WHETHER YOU MEANT TO OR *NOT*, YOU HELPED ME THROUGH A HARD TIME, HELPED ME FIND MY FEET...

... AT LEAST I *THINK* YOU DID.

YOU KNOW, HE *TOLD* ME... ABOUT WHAT YOU DID...

... THAT MAN *KILLED* ALL THOSE WOMEN, AND YOU *STILL* TRIED TO HELP HIM. IT'S AMAZING.

YEAH, WELL... YOU'D HAVE DONE THE SAME THING. AND REALLY, HE WASN'T COMPLETELY RESPONSIBLE...

SO... HOW DOES IT *FEEL*, SELINA KYLE? TO HELP AND NOT JUST TAKE?

I'M NOT SURE... *GOOD*, I GUESS... BUT *STRANGE*...

WHAT DO YOU MEAN?

IT'S HARD TO *SAY*... KIND OF *OVERWHELMING*, I GUESS. LIKE I'M WORRIED THAT I'LL FAIL.

AND I'M NOT USED TO FEELING THAT WAY.

I AM...

CLINIC

... DON'T *WORRY*, SELINA, YOU'LL DO JUST FINE.

And you know what? I think maybe she's right. Because for a long time all I could think about was pain-- my own and my family's. And that pain defined who I was, and ultimately just caused more...

Until there was nothing left for me beyond that.

But today I'm not thinking about the crooked cops and politicians. I'm not thinking about the wife-beaters and rapists, the mobsters...

SMILE

I'll get to them all, eventually.

No, right now, all I can think about is how good I'm going to feel when that sun goes down...

Finally, write down your favorite number, then look at the interpretation below...

25

This will define your priorities in life.

Cow signifies CAREER

Tiger signifies PRIDE

Sheep signifies LOVE

Horse signifies FAMILY

Pig signifies MONEY

Your description of dog implies YOUR OWN PERSONALITY. Your description of cat implies the personality of your partner. Your description of rat implies the personality of your enemies. Your description of coffee is how you interpret SEX. Your description of the Sea implies your own life.

...OH, IS *THAT* WHAT I THINK ABOUT SEX, huh?

Yellow: Someone you will never forget.

Orange: Someone you consider to be your friend.

Red: Someone that you really love.

White: Your twin soul.

Green: Someone that you will remember for the rest of your life.

huh... WEIRD...

To be blessed with good fortune, you must send this message to as many persons as your favorite number—

OH, THAT *SUCKS!* NO *WAY!*

THE HELL WITH THAT...

WHAT ARE YOU DOING, HOLLY?

ONE OF THOSE STUPID E-MAIL CHAIN LETTERS...

I CAN'T BELIEVE YOU STILL FILL THOSE OUT... BETWEEN CHAIN-MAIL AND ADS FOR PORN...

... I CAN HARDLY BEAR TO CHECK MY E-MAIL AT ALL...

I KNOW. I'M JUST A LITTLE MORE SUPERSTITIOUS THAN YOU, I GUESS...

WHO WAS THIS ONE FROM?

BELIEVE IT OR NOT, THE DALAI LAMA...

YOU'RE KIDDING? THE DALAI LAMA'S WORKING THE CHAIN LETTER SCAM NOW? BOY, EASTERN RELIGION IS SLIPPING...

Your description of coffee is how you interpret SEX.

Drugs.

WHAT'S THE DEAL?

NOTHING, I SHOULD JUST GET TO WORK, THAT'S ALL.

UH HUHH...

AND THAT'S WHY YOU JUST POURED A CUP OF COFFEE...

...LEFT IT ON THE COUNTER, AND THEN STALKED ACROSS THE ROOM.

WHAT? I CHANGED MY MIND... IT'S NOTHING.

IF THERE'S SOMETHING YOU WANT TO TALK ABOUT, YOU KNOW--

I KNOW...JUST DON'T WORRY ABOUT IT, SELINA. I'VE JUST GOT A LOT ON MY MIND RIGHT NOW...

I'LL SEE YA LATER.

WHY AM I GREEN?

And I just can't stop seeing these streets in junkie-vision.

We're so high!

Casual user

I'm a dealer. I'm a dealer

I'm a junkie.

Or noticing how easy it would be to give in...

JOINTS, ROCK, SKAG...

JOINTS, ROCK, SKAG...

Dealer.

Dealer.

So, while I'm really glad you helped me get off these streets, you also put me right back out on them...

"Pretending to be the same person I used to be.

Being your undercover agent... or whatever I am.

ARE YOU... uh... YOU KNOW?

SORRY, I'M ON A BREAK...

WHAT THE HELL IS THAT SUPPOSED TO MEAN?

FIGURE IT OUT, EINSTEIN.

Still, I guess it beats working... And there are certain perks to being out on the street.

WOODY'S DELICATESSEN

Woody
DEI

Red: Someone that you really love.

red-Karon

NO PLACE... CAN YOU TAKE A BREAK?

OKAY IF I TAKE OFF FOR A MINUTE, WOODY?

SURE, K-- IT'S PRETTY DEAD ANYWAY.

--AND THEN THE GUY ACTUALLY HAS THE NERVE TO ASK FOR HIS CHANGE...

YEAH, PEOPLE STINK...

NO, JUST CUSTOMERS... CUSTOMERS STINK.

SO WHAT'S UP WITH YOU? I HAVEN'T SEEN YOU FOR ALMOST A WEEK...

YEAH, I KNOW. I'VE JUST BEEN REALLY BUSY WITH THIS WORK I'VE BEEN DOING FOR MY FRIEND...

THE JOB YOU CAN'T TALK ABOUT, RIGHT?

YEAH, BUT NOT BECAUSE IT'S ILLEGAL... I ALWAYS TOLD YOU ABOUT ALL MY ILLEGAL ACTIVITIES.

I KNOW. THAT'S WHAT'S GOT ME WORRIED... WHAT THE HELL ARE YOU DOING, HOLLY?

I TOLD YOU,
I CAN'T--

HEY,
HOLLY!

THAT GUY YOU
WERE ASKIN' ABOUT? THE
DEALER GUY?

I GOT AN ADDRESS IF
YOU'RE STILL LOOKIN'...

OH, YEAH,
THANKS A LOT,
JENNI...

LET
ME KNOW
IF HIS STUFF IS
WORTH IT,
OKAY?

YEAH, UH...
NO PROBLEM.

STOP
IT. RIGHT
NOW.

YOU TOLD ME YOU
QUIT. GOD, I CAN'T BELIEVE
WHAT A SUCKER I AM...
I MEAN--

IT'S NOT WHAT YOU THINK,
OKAY? THIS IS PART OF WHAT
I'M DOING... MY JOB.

OH,
RIGHT...
IT'S YOUR
JOB TO
SCORE
HEROIN,
HUH?

What the
hell am I
supposed
to do now,
Selina?

Of course, if I do tell her, I don't have to tell her the whole truth, do I?

OKAY, LISTEN... HAVE YOU EVER READ SHERLOCK HOLMES?

WHAT?

SHERLOCK HOLMES, HAVE YOU EVER READ ANY OF THEM?

YEAH, SURE, BUT WHAT'S *THAT* GOT TO DO WITH ANYTHING?

REMEMBER HOW HOLMES ALWAYS HAD A BUNCH OF LOCAL KIDS WORKING FOR HIM...

...GETTING INTO PLACES HE COULDN'T GO?

YEAH, THE BAKER STREET DOZEN OR SOMETHING LIKE THAT.

THAT'S SORT OF WHAT *I* AM... THE EAST END HAS SOMEBODY WATCHING IT NOW, AND SOME OF US ARE *WORKING* FOR THAT PERSON.

BUT YOU HAVE'TA KEEP THIS A *SECRET*, DO YOU UNDERSTAND?

ARE YOU *SERIOUS?* WHO IS IT?

BATMAN?

NO, AND I CAN'T TELL YOU ANY MORE THAN I ALREADY HAVE.

AND YOU *STILL* HAVEN'T ANSWERED ME YET. DO YOU UNDERSTAND WHAT IT *MEANS*, THAT I'M TELLING YOU THIS?

YEAH, IT MEANS I'M PART OF YOUR *SECRET* NOW, I GUESS.

ASSUMING YOU'RE NOT FULL OF IT.

YOU *KNOW* I CAN'T LIE TO YOU.

Secrets are a strange thing.

They can be like a trap, or a weight, when you have to keep someone else's...

...They can grow inside you, making you sick.

But sometimes they can be like a bond.

And those times they can be kinda cool.

DAVID G.
814 42ND
2ND FLOOR

Glue Sniffers.

Cruising for drugs.

Addict/ Hooker.

A lot of the job is just waiting, which is something I know really well...

It seems like my whole life has been nothing but waiting sometimes...

Me and Davey, in the dark, waiting for dad to stop yelling at mom...

And the quiet times, waiting for one of us to do something that would make him snap.

Then later, living on the streets—that was a whole different kind of waiting...

It was like passing the time, waiting for life to really begin. Living in between the moments.

And I guess I just couldn't take it, so I copped out.

I didn't think that at the time, I thought I was saving myself but hindsight is 20-20.

There I was just waiting for the revelation that would get me to leave.

And then it was back on the streets, and on to new problems. And a whole new definition of waiting.

And when you're a junkie that's all you do—

Wait to score, wait to shoot up, wait for it to wear off, wait for a guy who gives you more money to score again, do anything he wants to get it, wait to score, wait to shoot up—

And then when you quit, it's all waiting to not see the world in junkie-vision, I guess...

Dealer

Holding

I wonder when that starts.

The nice thing about this new relationship with Selina is that even though I still have a lot of waiting to do...

...at least now I feel useful.

I can use all my life experience to my advantage for a change...

And that makes me feel stronger... Prouder.

Tiger signifies PRIDE.

David G. is a new dealer in the neighborhood who I've been hearing about—An up-and-comer from the sound of it.

80% Baby Laxative

He's supposed to be seriously connected and pretty dangerous.

Undercover Cop.

Pre-op trainee.

Wannabe Gang Banger

Nodding off.

But I have yet to lay eyes on this dude.

Farrah-Junkie

HEY, FARRAH, WHAT'S UP?

HOLLY? DAMN, I AIN'T SEEN YOU FOR MONTHS, GIRL...

GET YERSELF A SUGAR DADDY?

NO, uh, NOT EXACTLY, um, LOOK...

I HEARD THAT DAVID G. WAS SELLING, BUT I DON'T KNOW HIM...

COULD YOU POINT HIM OUT?

GOT IT BAD, DON'TCHA, GIRL? YEAH, DAVID G. BE RIGHT OVER THERE...

ASK ME, THO, HE AIN'T ALL THAT...

No way. No way. That guy is a cop.

I am not wrong about this. He's good. I'll give him that, but he can't stop being a cop underneath it.

And I learned too much in the early Catwoman days to miss spotting a narc.

Damn. What do I do now?

OUTTA THE WAY, WOMAN!

HEY!

Where the hell is he going in such a hurry?

He's just going to disappear. Damn it, what should I do?

Think, Holly...

I don't think Selina would mind me borrowing a car for a good cause.

But I'm not going to tell her, just in case.

WELL, I DIDN'T *KNOW* HE WAS A COP WHEN I STARTED LOOKING INTO HIM, BUT *NOW* HE JUST SEEMS SUSPICIOUS...

YOU'RE NOT SUPPOSED TO BE GETTING IN THIS DEEP, HOLLY...

I CAN TAKE CARE OF MYSELF, SELINA.

THAT'S NOT THE POINT.

LOOK, JUST GET OVER HERE, OKAY? THIS GUY COULD LEAD TO BIGGER THINGS.

I'LL KEEP AN EYE ON HIM.

sheesh... WHAT A NAG.

--YEAH, I KNOW... WHAT AM *I* SUPPOSED TO DO ABOUT IT? I MEAN, YOU PAGE ME WITH A 911 WHEN I'M ON THE *JOB*-- THAT'S *BUNK.*

I DON'T THINK YOU'RE *UNDERSTANDING* ME, OFFICER...

OH, I UNDERSTAND YOU... BUT I'M NOT HEARING *ANY* OF THIS.

MY INVESTIGATION LEADS WHERE IT *LEADS*.

Damn it. Just more cops... This whole night has been a waste of time.

PLEASE, LET'S BE *REASONABLE* HERE... HAVE A SEAT AND WE CAN DISCUSS IT.

THERE'S *NOTHING* TO DISCUSS, MACNULTY... I'M NOT INTERESTED IN YOUR *GAME*, WHATEVER IT IS...

THAT'S REALLY *TOO BAD*, OFFICER...

...FOR YOU.

KA-RASH!!

Tiger signifies PRIDE.

JUST WHAT THE HELL D'YOU THINK YOU'RE DOIN'?

YOU HEAR "FREEZE POLICE" AND YOU DON'T KEEP RUNNIN', GIRL.

UNLESS YOU WANNA END UP SHOT...

NOT THAT IT MATTERS NOW, I GUESS.

SO, YOU WANNA GET SARGE'S CLEARANCE FIRST OR WHAT?

NAH, THIS STUPID TWIST IS A BLESSING IN DISGUISE--THE WAY I SEE IT, SHE MUST'VE BEEN HERE TO SCORE FROM OLD DAVID G.--

--BUT SOMEHOW SHE FIGURED HE WAS A COP...

"SO SHE MUST'VE SHOT HIM.

LUCKILY, WE ARRIVED IN TIME TO PREVENT THE SUSPECT'S ESCAPE...

"IT'S JUST TOO BAD SHE WAS KILLED WHILE RESISTING ARREST.

NICE STORY...

HOLLY... DAMN IT...

OKAY, IT'S GONNA BE OKAY...

'BOUT TIME... I ALMOST HAD TO HANDLE THOSE GUYS MYSELF...

OKAY, JUST HOLD ON, HOLLY... I'M GONNA GET YOU SOME HELP RIGHT NOW...

"...THEY KILLED THAT GUY...

"...THE NARC..."

NOT NOW. YOU CAN TELL ME LATER... FIRST WE'VE GOTTA GET YOU OUT OF HERE...

WHHEEOOOWHHEEOOO

DAMN IT... DAMN.

OOWHEEOOO

"...TRY THE CONVERTIBLE... WORKED FOR ME...

WHAT?

SORRY TO GET YOU UP, LESLIE... I JUST DIDN'T KNOW WHERE ELSE TO GO...

DON'T GIVE IT A SECOND THOUGHT, THIS IS WHAT I'M *HERE* FOR...

SHE'S GOING TO BE *OKAY*, RIGHT?

I THINK SO...NEED TO GET A *CLOSER LOOK*...

DOESN'T APPEAR TO HAVE HIT THE *ARTERY*.

LET ME JUST GIVE HER SOMETHING FOR THE *PAIN* RIGHT NOW.

NO. SELINA, SHE'S IN A LOT OF PAIN, AND IT'S GOING TO GET *WORSE* IN A MINUTE.

SHE CAN'T HAVE *NARCOTICS*... SHE'S A RECOVERING ADDICT.

OH, I SEE...

IT'S JUST... Y'KNOW... IT'S MY FAULT. SHE WORKS FOR ME.

SHE'S MY FRIEND.

I KNOW, SELINA.

WOULD YOU RATHER STAY?

NO, I'VE GOT TO DITCH THIS CAR AND FIND OUT WHAT THE HELL IS GOING ON...

JUST TAKE CARE OF HER, LESLIE...

SHE'S JUST ABOUT ALL I'VE GOT.

I'M AFRAID THIS IS GOING TO HURT, DEAR...

--HELL'RE *YOU* DOIN' ON THIS SIDE OF THE TOWN, *ALLEN?* THIS AIN'T EXACTLY YOUR *BEAT...*

I KNOW IT, MacNALTY, AND DON'T THINK I'M ANY TOO HAPPY TO BE HERE.

BUT, FACT IS, THIS IS THE *THIRD UNDERCOVER AGENT* KILLED IN THE EAST END IN LESS THAN A YEAR.

...SO LIEUTENANT SAWYER THOUGHT IT BEST IF SOMEONE FROM OUTSIDE THE AREA LOOKED INTO IT.

THOUGHT A LITTLE *PERSPECTIVE* MIGHT HELP OUT, I GUESS.

SHEESH... WHY DIDN'T HE JUST SEND IN I. A. IN THAT CASE?

OH, STOP BEIN' A *CRYBABY...* I'M NOT GONNA STEP ON YOUR TOES.

SO, YOU WANNA GIVE ME THE *RUNDOWN* HERE?

SURE... ...WE GOT A CALL TO MEET THE VIC AT THIS LOCATION. APPARENTLY HE HAD A *TIP* FOR US...

...BUT JUST AS WE'RE ABOUT TO ENTER, WE HEAR A *SHOT*.

WE ENTER, GUNS DRAWN-- FIND OUR MAN ON THE FLOOR WITH HIS BRAINS BLOWN OUT AND SOME *CHICK* RUNNING OUT THE BACK.

FARLEY AND RICKETT GIVE PURSUIT, WINGING THE SUSPECT.

BUT APPARENTLY SHE HAD SOME PRETTY *SERIOUS* BACKUP HIDING IN THE ALLEY.

TOOK DOWN TWO OF MY BEST MEN IN *SECONDS*, AND THEN DISAPPEARED WITH THE CHICK.

YEAH, YOU *GOTTA* LOVE GOTHAM FOR *THAT,* DON'TCHA?

WHAT'D YOUR *MEN* SAY? THEY GIVE A DESCRIPTION?

OF THE *SHOOTER,* YEAH... ...BUT WHOEVER KNOCKED 'EM AROUND? NAH, THEY DIDN'T SEE SQUAT.

WHY AM I NOT SURPRISED?

...uh... YEAH...

GOOD THINKING...

YOU *KNOW*, SELINA, IF YOU'RE GONNA *POP IN* YOU SHOULD TRY TO MAKE IT ABOUT FOUR HOURS EARLIER NEXT TIME.

YEAH, I'LL KEEP IT IN *MIND*, SLAM...

...NOW GET SOME CLOTHES ON AND WE CAN GET TO WORK.

WORK, hunh? YOU KEEP SOME PRETTY CRUDDY HOURS, LADY.

WHATEVER...

HEY--*NICE* BOXERS.

DO I MAKE FUN OF *YOUR* OUTFIT? NO.

AND I *COULD*, TOO, BELIEVE ME.

--BUD, NO I'N TOO PORITE F'R DAT.

SO, FUN AND GAMES ASIDE, I TAKE IT THIS IS *SERIOUS*?

YEAH, I WOULDN'T BE HERE OTHERWISE... HOLLY'S HURT. SHE GOT SHOT.

WHAT *HAPPENED*?

I'M NOT EXACTLY SURE...

SHE WAS SUPPOSED TO BE FOLLOWING SOME DEALER, BUT THEN SHE CALLS ME AND SAYS HE'S A *NARC*, BUT THAT SHE'S FOLLOWING HIM *ANYWAY*.

HE WAS *MEETING* SOMEONE, I GUESS.

WHEN I SHOWED UP SHE'D *ALREADY* TAKEN A BULLET AND THESE TWO PIGS WERE ABOUT TO FINISH THE JOB.

I DON'T REALLY KNOW WHAT HAPPENED *IN BETWEEN*, BUT SHE SAID THEY'D *KILLED* THE NARC...

AM I UNDERSTANDING THIS RIGHT? THESE GUYS ARE *COPS*?

AND THEY *KILLED* ANOTHER COP?

LIKE I SAID, I'M NOT SURE.

ALL I KNOW IS WHAT HOLLY TOLD ME AND THAT THEY TRIED TO *KILL HER*. IT WASN'T LIKE I COULD GO BACK AND POKE AROUND, THE PLACE WOULD'VE BEEN *SWARMING* WITH COPS BY THEN.

YEAH... SO YOU WANT ME TO DIG AROUND A LITTLE?

WELL, YOU *SAID* YOU WERE WORKING ON A CASE AGAINST THE G.C.P.D.* -- THIS WOULD SEEM TO TIE IN PRETTY WELL...

*--ISSUE#5.

I CAN *PAY YOU* FOR YOUR TIME, SLAM... MONEY'S *NOT* A PROBLEM.

I CAN'T TAKE YOUR MONEY, SELINA...

BESIDES, YOU MADE THE COFFEE, ANYWAY.

BEEN A LONG TIME SINCE A BEAUTIFUL WOMAN MADE ME COFFEE IN THE MIDDLE OF THE NIGHT.

YOU TIDY UP THIS PLACE AND YOU MIGHT HAVE BETTER LUCK WITH THE LADIES.

OH, IS *THAT* RIGHT?

SO THEN... YOU'LL *HELP?*

HOW COULD I SAY NO?

LEMME JUST MAKE A PHONE CALL... I'VE GOT A *SOURCE* THAT MIGHT BE ABLE TO SHED SOME LIGHT ON THE EVENING'S *ACTIVITIES...*

--LEMME JUST HAVE A WORD WITH THE LIEUTENANT, ALLEN, AND I'LL BE RIGHT BACK...

GCPD
PRECINCT HOUSE 14

TAKE YOUR TIME, SERGEANT.

RING, RING

DETECTIVES, FARRUCCI HERE.

OH, GIVE ME A BREAK, IT'S THE MIDDLE OF THE DAMN NIGHT...

...YEAH YEAH,...ALL RIGHT. GIMME A HALF HOUR.

UNBELIEVABLE, MY MOTHER-IN-LAW NEEDS ME TO PICK UP HER PRESCRIPTION AT THIS HOUR.

YEAH, IT'S ALWAYS SOMETHING, ISN'T IT?

WITH THIS WOMAN IT IS...

DON'T LET MACNALTY YANK YOUR CHAIN TOO MUCH, ALLEN.

NOT TO WORRY, DETECTIVE FARRUCCI, I'VE HANDLED HIS TYPE BEFORE.

-- I MEAN HOW AM I SUPPOSED TO DO ANYTHING WITH THIS M.C.U. INTERLOPER NOSING AROUND?

WHAT DO YOU *WANT* FROM ME, SERGEANT? IF THE CHIEF OF POLICE WANTS A DETECTIVE FROM *MAJOR CRIMES* LOOKING INTO SOMETHING, I CAN'T EXACTLY SAY *NO*, NOW, CAN I?

OKAY, BUT DOES HE HAVETA BE SO FAR DOWN MY *THROAT*? ISN'T THERE ANYONE *ELSE* IN THE SQUAD WHO CAN BABYSIT THIS SNOOP?

NO... I WANT *YOU* TO DO THIS, MacNALTY, BECAUSE *YOU'RE* THE ONE THAT SCREWED UP... AND *YOU'RE* THE ONE THAT'S GONNA STOP THIS DETECTIVE ALLEN FROM FINDING OUT ANYTHING.

ARE WE *CLEAR*?

YEAH, WE'RE CLEAR...

YOU GOT ANY IDEAS ON FINDING YOUR WITNESS?

YOU MEAN OUR *SUSPECT*, DON'T YOU?

RIGHT.

YEAH, I *THINK* I'VE GOT IT UNDER CONTROL...

WHO'S YOUR *FRIEND*, BRADLEY?

East Side Diner

OPEN 24 HRS

I THOUGHT THIS WAS GONNA BE JUST YOU AND ME...

IT'S *OKAY*, FARRUCCI, I'LL VOUCH FOR HER.

SHE GOT A *NAME?*

I'M *SELINA*, DETECTIVE, AND AND I REALLY APPRECIATE YOU MEETING US LIKE THIS...

YEAH, THAT'S ALL RIGHT...

SO ANYWAY, WHAT'S THE *DEAL*, BRADLEY?

UNLESS I'M MISTAKEN, YOU GUYS LOST AN *UNDERCOVER COP* TONIGHT, RIGHT?

YEAH... BUT THE BRASS'RE SITTIN' ON IT FOR NOW, BUT IT'LL BE ALL OVER THE NEWS IN THE MORNING.

I MEAN, THESE UNDERCOVER GUYS KNOW THE RISKS, I GUESS, BUT--

AND WHAT IF I WAS TO TELL YOU THAT THIS GUY WAS ACTUALLY SHOT BY *COPS,* NOT *CROOKS?*

DAMN IT, BRADLEY, YOU DRAG ME OUT IN THE MIDDLE OF THE NIGHT FOR *MORE* OF THIS *GARBAGE?* I OUGHTTA--

HE'S TELLING THE *TRUTH.* A FRIEND OF MINE *SAW* IT.

DAMN IT TO *HELL.*

LEMME TELL YOU A LITTLE STORY... UNDERSTANDING THAT WE *NEVER* HAD THIS CONVERSATION, OF COURSE.

NATURALLY.

"ABOUT SIX MONTHS AGO, SOME KIND OF *TURF WAR* WENT DOWN IN THE EAST END...

"IT WAS KEPT PRETTY QUIET, BUT A *LOT* OF BLOOD SPILLED.

"EVERY TWO DAYS, ANOTHER CORNER WAS GETTING SHOT UP.

"AND OF COURSE, NO ONE *EVER* SAW ANYTHING.

YOU *OBVIOUSLY* DON'T THINK THIS GUY *OFFED* HIMSELF.

NO. BUT *NO ONE* WAS IN THE OBSERVATION ROOM WHEN I WAS *INTERROGATING* THAT PERP... SO IF THEY KILLED HIM, THEN THE WHOLE PLACE IS *BUGGED...*

BUT THING IS, IF IT'S WHAT I THINK--THAT THERE ARE A BUNCH OF *DIRTY COPS* WORKING FOR SOMEONE WHO WANTED CONTROL OF THE EAST END DRUG TRADE...

WELL, IF THAT'S TRUE, IT GOES UP *TOO HIGH.*

THAT'S WHY I LET IT *DROP*, BRADLEY... BECAUSE IF I LOOK INTO IT TOO HARD, *I* COULD END UP JUST LIKE THAT KID IN LOCK-UP.

AND I'VE GOT A WIFE AND KIDS TO THINK OF...

I *KNOW* YOU WANNA NAIL THESE GUYS, SLAM, AND BELIEVE ME, I'D LOVE TO SEE IT HAPPEN...

...BUT IF YOU WANT *MY* ADVICE...

I'D LET IT GO.

AND AS FAR AS YOUR *FRIEND* GOES, MISS... WELL, I'D TELL HER TO JUST *FORGET* WHATEVER IT WAS SHE SAW...

...AND PRAY TO GOD NO ONE SAW HER, TOO.

IT DOESN'T LOOK LIKE THERE'LL BE ANY PERMANENT DAMAGE. SHE WAS LUCKY.

NOT SO LUCKY AS SOME.

NO, I GUESS NOT, BUT SHE'LL *SURVIVE*, AND A LOT DON'T... NOW, LET'S LET HER GET SOME REST, SHALL WE?

SO, DID YOU FIND YOUR ANSWERS?

SORT OF... BUT IT LOOKS LIKE A PROBLEM THAT COULD BE TOO BIG FOR US TO SOLVE ON OUR OWN RIGHT NOW.

I *STILL* SAY WE TAKE THEM DOWN.

I CAN *BARELY* STAND HONEST COPS, BUT *DIRTY* ONES...

I KNOW, SLAM, BUT WE'VE GOT TO THINK ABOUT HOLLY NOW.

SHE'S LYING ON THAT BED BECAUSE OF ME, OKAY?

IF THIS GOES ANY FURTHER, SHE COULD GET IN *REAL* TROUBLE...

ANY WITNESS THAT COMES FORWARD WITH *ANYTHING*--

--IS JUST GOING TO BE ANOTHER *TARGET.*

I *KNOW,* BUT WHAT ELSE ARE WE SUPPOSED TO DO? WE SUPPOSED TO JUST LET IT CONTINUE?

LOOK, MAYBE WE DON'T *NEED* HER INVOLVED IN THIS ANYWAY. WE JUST HAVE TO SET A *TRAP* FOR THESE--

WAIT! I THINK YOU'D BETTER SEE THIS...

--AND THIS POLICE SKETCH OF THE PRIME SUSPECT IN THE BRUTAL MURDER OF A GOTHAM POLICE OFFICER WORKING UNDERCOVER--

--HAS JUST BEEN RELEASED.

KGOH

IF ANYONE HAS *ANY* INFORMATION ABOUT THE IDENTITY OR THE WHEREABOUTS OF THIS YOUNG WOMAN, PLEASE CALL THE NUMBER ON THE SCREEN.

1-800-URBUSTE

WELL, I GUESS THE DECISION'S BEEN TAKEN OUT OF OUR HANDS...

GOTHAM CITY, THE EAST END.

--PROBABLY *HEARD* ABOUT IT. BEEN ON THE NEWS SINCE YESTERDAY MORNING...

...UNDERCOVER COP GOT *KILLED,* AND SHE WAS SEEN FLEEING THE SCENE OF THE CRIME.

NOW WE'RE OUT POUNDING THE PAVEMENT TO SEE IF ANYONE KNOWS WHO THIS GIRL *IS*...

ARMED AND DANGEROUS
IF YOU SEE THIS WOMAN, PLEASE CALL
1-800-UBBUSTED

SO, DOES SHE RING ANY BELLS?

NO... I DON'T THINK I'VE SEEN HER AROUND HERE...

UH, YEAH... LIKE *KARON* HERE SAYS, SHE DOESN'T LOOK FAMILIAR...

OKAY, WELL, I'M GONNA LEAVE THIS HERE... YOU MIND POSTING IT? MAYBE ONE OF YOUR CUSTOMERS'LL RECOGNIZE HER?

MODIGLIANI

OH, SURE... OF COURSE, OFFICER.

NOT TO WORRY... I'M *WAY* AHEAD OF YOU, SLAM.

matt hollingsworth
-colorist-

willie schubert
-letterer-

ed brubaker
-writer-

brad rader
-penciller-

rick burchett
-inker-

lysa hawkins
-associate editor-

matt idelson
-editor-

ANY IDEA WHO KAREN IS?

IT'S KAR-*ON*... WITH AN O. SHE'S HOLLY'S GIRLFRIEND, I THINK.

WHY?

SHE LEFT A MESSAGE... SOUNDS A BIT FREAKED. GUESS THE COPS ARE PEDDLING THAT *SKETCH* ALL OVER TOWN...

WELL, IF EVERYTHING GOES AS *PLANNED*, SHE WON'T HAVE ANYTHING TO WORRY ABOUT IN A DAY OR TWO...

YEAH, WE'LL *SEE*, I GUESS...

YOU'RE NOT STARTING TO HAVE *DOUBTS*, ARE YOU?

HEY, I'VE *BEEN* HAVING DOUBTS SINCE YOU CAME UP WITH THIS COCKAMAMIE IDEA YESTERDAY.

MY LACK OF *SLEEP* SINCE THEN IS JUST MAKING THEM MORE *OBVIOUS*.

LOOK, THERE'RE ONLY A FEW MORE DETAILS TO PUT INTO PLACE NOW.

SO YOU'RE JUST GOING TO HAVE TO *TRUST ME*, SLAM...

...I'VE BEEN PULLING OFF SCHEMES LIKE THIS SINCE I WAS A TEENAGER.

BESIDES, EVEN IF IT DOESN'T WORK, IT'LL PROBABLY *STILL* DRAW SOME OF THE HEAT OFF *HOLLY*...AND *THAT'S* WHAT WE'RE DOING THIS FOR.

WELL, THAT MAKES ME FEEL A LOT BETTER...

I know you think what we're planning is *dangerous*, Slam, and it is...

But so am I... and it's about time I reminded our *enemies* of that.

I was prepared to let this all go...

But these crooked cops hurt my friend, and now they're using her as their *scapegoat*...

So, as far as I'm concerned, they let the lion out of the cage.

Now they have to suffer the consequences.

--JUST LIKE I TOLD YOU, ALLEN, THAT PLACE WAS A DEAD END.

Hrk Hrk!

I FOLLOW ALL LEADS, SERGEANT MacNALTY, THAT'S HOW I WORK.

'SCUSE ME FOR A MINUTE, WOULD'JA?

SURE. TAKE YOUR TIME...

NICE JOB, MORONS... WHY DON'T YOU BE A LITTLE MORE OBVIOUS?

SORRY, SARGE... WE JUST DIDN'T KNOW WHAT TO DO ABOUT TONIGHT...

I MEAN, ARE YOU GONNA BE ABLE TO DITCH THE M.C.U. SNITCH IN TIME?

Y'KNOW WHAT? WHEN PLANS CHANGE, I'LL BE THE ONE TO TELL YOU, OKAY?

UNLESS YOU HEAR DIFFERENTLY, ASSUME EVERY-THING IS ON SCHEDULE.

NOW, DID YOU GET THE KEYS FOR THE MOBILE TRANSPORT YET, RICKETT?

NO, SARGE, WE WERE WAITING TO HEAR FROM YOU, LIKE I SAID...

WELL, I GUESS YOU BETTER GET OFF YOUR BUTT, THEN, HADN'T YOU?

SURE, SARGE... SURE... DON'T SWEAT IT...

AND YOU *BOTH* BETTER JUST KEEP YOUR EYES OPEN FOR WHOEVER IT WAS THAT CLEANED YOUR CLOCKS THE OTHER NIGHT.

WHAT WAS ALL THAT ABOUT?

AH, NOTHIN'... THEY'RE JUST PLANNIN' A SURPRISE PARTY FOR THE LIEUTENANT...

OH YEAH, HE GOT A BIRTHDAY COMIN' UP?

SOMETHING LIKE THAT...

OKAY, HERE WE GO...

EXCUSE ME, OFFICER?

YEAH?

I THINK I'VE GOT SOMETHING YOU *MIGHT* FIND INTERESTING...

east side PAWN and LOAN

SNIKT

SMAK!

"...JEEZ, I REALLY GOTTA START TAKIN' A BIGGER STINKIN' CUT OF 'SOMMA THIS ACTION...

"...THESE SUCKERS'R TAKIN' ADVANTAGE OF MY GENEROUS NATURE...

WELL, I HOPE YOU SAVED UP SOME OF THAT GENEROSITY FOR *ME*, JEFFO...

...OR WE COULD HAVE A PROBLEM.

WHAT THE HELL...? CATWOMAN?

SO THE RUMORS 'RE TRUE, YOU'RE BACK... WHATTA YA GOT, BABY? I KNOW IT'S GOTTA BE GOOD.

TIMES'VE CHANGED, JEFFO... I'M NOT SELLING.

I'M HERE BECAUSE I NEED SOME INFORMATION.

INFORMATION, huh? ABOUT WHAT?

I SPENT THE LAST DAY AND A HALF TURNING OVER ROCKS--

--TO FIND OUT EVERYTHING I COULD ABOUT THIS CROOKED REGIME OF COPS IN THE EAST END RIGHT NOW...

...SO, I KNOW THERE'S A MAJOR DROP GOING DOWN TONIGHT THAT THEY'RE INVOLVED IN...

WHAT I DON'T KNOW IS: WHERE?

YOU'RE OUT OF YOUR MIND, GIRLIE... I AIN'T BREATHIN' A WORD ABOUT NONE A'THAT.

THAT *ISN'T* AN OPTION!

AHH! JACKO!

SORRY, JACKO CAN'T PLAY RIGHT NOW, HE'S TAKING A NAP...

NOW, ARE YOU GONNA *TALK* OR DOES THIS HAVE TO GET *UGLY*?

ALL RIGHT... ALL RIGHT...

I'M A *BUSINESS-MAN*, AFTER ALL...

BUT I AIN'T JUST *GIVIN'* THIS KINDA INFO AWAY...

OKAY THEN, LET'S MAKE A *DEAL*... WHAT DO YOU WANT?

ACTUALLY, THERE IS SOMETHING THAT YOU WOULDN'T EVEN REALLY HAVE'TA GO OUTTA YER WAY FOR IF YER GOIN' UP AGAINST THESE MUGS ANYWAY...

WHAT A SURPRISE...

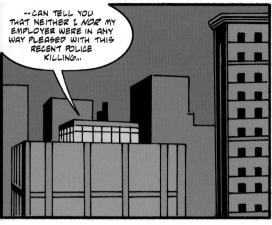

--CAN TELL YOU THAT NEITHER I *NOR* MY EMPLOYER WERE IN ANY WAY PLEASED WITH THIS RECENT POLICE KILLING...

WE REALLY DON'T WANT TO DRAW SO MUCH ATTENTION TO OUR ACTIVITIES IN THE EAST END.

I KNOW, MY MEN HAVE BEEN REPRIMANDED, AND SERGEANT MacNALTY IS HANDLING THE OUTSIDE INVESTIGATOR *PERSONALLY*.

MacNALTY'S A *GOOD* MAN FOR THAT KIND OF DUPLICITY, I'D THINK...

...IT'S QUITE IN HIS NATURE.

I SUPPOSE SO, ALONG WITH AN ASSORTMENT OF OTHER BAD QUALITIES.

AND DID YOUR MEN HAVE ANYTHING MORE TO SAY ABOUT WHO IT WAS THAT *ATTACKED* THEM BEFORE THEY COULD GET RID OF THEIR WITNESS?

HELL, IN THIS CITY WHO *KNOWS?* COULD'VE BEEN BATMAN, ROBIN OR THE FREAKIN' HUNTRESS...

I HEAR THERE'S EVEN A NEW *BATGIRL* OUT THERE, TOO...

LET'S NOT FORGET *CATWOMAN*...

"...RECENT EVENTS HAVE SHOWN THAT HER AGENDA IS NOT WHAT IT USED TO BE.

I SUPPOSE SHE IS A POSSIBILITY, BUT IT SEEMS LIKE A STRETCH TO ME...

I MEAN, THIS WAS WAY OUT IN THE INDUSTRIAL AREA, WHAT WOULD SHE EVEN BE DOING THERE?

IT'S A MOOT POINT, REALLY... BUT ONE THING IS CERTAIN...

...TONIGHT'S TRANSACTION NEEDS TO GO OFF WITHOUT A HITCH, SO YOUR MEN HAD BETTER BE READY FOR ANY EVENTUALITY...

...EVEN BATMAN.

OH, BELIEVE ME, THEY ARE.

WE ALL KNOW HOW IMPORTANT THIS DELIVERY IS TO THE BIG BOSS...

...THEY'RE GOING IN LIKE IT WAS THE BLITZ...

WELL, THEN, YOU'D BETTER HOPE THAT'S GOOD ENOUGH.

SO, ANY WORD ON THE *SQUIRT?*

SHE'S DOING GOOD... LESLIE SAID THE COPS WERE AROUND EARLIER, ASKING IF SHE'D TREATED ANY GUNSHOT WOUNDS BUT SHE GOT RID OF THEM.

SHE'S A *CLASSY LADY,* THAT DOCTOR THOMPKINS.

WELL, WHEN THIS IS ALL OVER MAYBE I'LL SEE IF I CAN'T FIX YOU TWO UP...

DON'T DO ME ANY *FAVORS,* OKAY? SHE'S NOT EXACTLY MY TYPE...

AND WHAT EXACTLY *IS* YOUR TYPE, PRAY TELL?

CAN WE *PLEASE* CHANGE THE SUBJECT? I THOUGHT WE WERE ON A *SCHEDULE...*

WE ARE, AND IT LOOKS LIKE WE'RE RIGHT ON TIME...

SEE THE MOBILE *G.C.P.D* UNIT UP AHEAD?

THAT'S THEM.

JEFFO DIDN'T KNOW THE *EXACT* LOCATION OF THE *SWAP,* BUT HE KNEW ABOUT THE TRANSPORT VAN, WHICH WAS *GOOD ENOUGH.*

OH MAN, THESE GUYS'VE GOT *BRASS ONES,* I'M TELLIN' YA...

TRUE, BUT AFTER TONIGHT, THEY'LL BE *LUCKY* IF THEY HAVE *ANY* AT ALL.

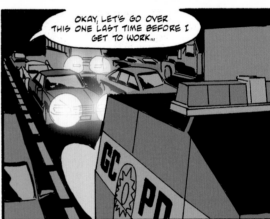

OKAY, LET'S GO OVER THIS ONE *LAST* TIME BEFORE I GET TO WORK...

THEY STILL BACK THERE?

YEAH, JUST LIKE HE SAID...

...ONE CAR LENGTH BEHIND, JUST IN CASE.

YEAH, LIKE *ANYONE'S* GONNA BE STUPID ENOUGH TO TAKE ON A *POLICE VAN...*

...EVEN WHEN IT'S CARRYING *200 POUNDS* OF *PURE GRADE SMACK.*

YOU THINK WHAT YOU *WANT,* FARLEY--

--I'LL STOP WORRYING WHEN WE *DROP* THIS JUNK OFF AND GET THE *PACKAGE.*

OKAY, I'M OUT... REMEMBER, WAIT FOR THE RIGHT MOMENT.

YEAH, YEAH... JUST BE *CAREFUL*.

I SWEAR TO GOD, IF THESE TWO SCREW THIS UP--

--AFTER THEY LET THAT CHICK GET AWAY THE OTHER NIGHT...

...I'M GONNA--

WHUMP

WHAT THE *HELL* WAS THAT?

Hunh... MUSTA BEEN A *PIGEON* OR SOMETHIN'!

Okay, Selina, you only get one shot at this.

What do you think? Three-second window, or four?

Let's hope it's four...

WHAT'RE THEY *DOING?* I SAID NOT TO GET OUT OF MY SIGHT...

Four...

Three...

Two...

One...

CHNNK

THESE GUYS...

...THEY'RE LOSING THE ABILITY TO FOLLOW ORDERS...

...LUCKY FOR THEM NOTHING HAPPENED THIS TIME.

YEAH, THIS IS A GREAT PLAN... REALLY GREAT...

--IT'S ALL AS MISTER KOSOV SAID IT WOULD BE...

TALK IS CHEAP, BORIS, LET'S SEE THE PACKAGE.

MY NAME IS *NOT BORIS*... IT IS *LUDVIG*...

WHATEVER... JUST GET ON WITH IT.

THIS SHOULD PROVE *ACCEPTABLE*, I BELIEVE.

28 MILLION IN DIAMONDS...

THAT WAS THE *AGREED UPON* FIGURE, WAS IT NOT?

SURE, IGOR. IT LOOKS LIKE IT'S ALL IN ORDER...

I'LL TAKE THE KEYS TO THE VAN NOW, AND A UNIFORM SO AS NOT TO ATTRACT ATTENTION.

YEAH... JUST GIMME A SECOND HERE...

CLIK !!!

OKAY, HERE YOU GO, ANTON, THE UNIFORM IS INSIDE... JUST LEAVE THE VAN--

DEET

THIS CANNOT BE...

COVER YOUR FACE!

THEY ARE ALL DESTROYED. VASILY WILL KILL ME...

I'M AFRAID I'M GOING TO REQUIRE THE RETURN OF THE PACKAGE...

ALL RIGHT... RICKETT, BETTER GIVE HIM BACK THE CASE...WE'LL SORT THIS OUT LATER.

WHAT *KEPT* YOU?

C'MON, RICKETT, GET IT OVER HERE!

WELL, DID YOU GET IT?

WHAT DO *YOU* THINK?

UH.... I THINK WE GOT A *PROBLEM*, SARGE...

GOTHAM CITY, THE EAST END.

--YEAH, I KNOW IT'S THE MIDDLE OF THE DAMN NIGHT, RENEE...

GCPD
PRECINCT HOUSE 14

"BUT WHAT AM I SUPPOSED TO DO? JUST LEAVE?

Nah, MacNALTY TOOK OFF A FEW HOURS AGO, SO I CAN FINALLY GET SOME WORK DONE...

YEAH, I'M PRETTY SURE HE IS. PROVING IT'S THE PROBLEM... SERGEANT MacNALTY SEEMS TO BE PRETTY GOOD AT COVERING HIS TRACKS...

RIGHT NOW? RIGHT NOW I'M DIGGING THROUGH SOME OLD FILES OF MacNALTY'S...

...SOME OF HIS CLOSED CASES ARE PRETTY FISHY...

YOU KNOW THE ROUTINE-- GUY CONFESSES TO MURDER, THEN OFFS HIMSELF IN THE HOLDING TANK THE NEXT DAY.

DECEASED

I KNOW... I KNOW... BUT HIS LIEUTENANT'S BEEN SIGNING OFF ON ALL OF HIS CASES, SO...

DECEASED

Uh huh... I'M AWARE OF THAT POSSIBILITY TOO, RENEE.

YES, I AM READY FOR TROUBLE IF I NEED TO BE.

LISTEN, STOP ACTING LIKE MY *MOM*, OKAY, MONTOYA?

JUST GIVE LIEUTENANT SAWYER THE LOWDOWN AND LET HER KNOW THIS MIGHT TAKE ANOTHER FEW DAYS...

OH REALLY, WHO THEY GOT YOU PARTNERING WITH UNTIL I GET BACK?

DRIVER? OH C'MON, HE'S NOT SO BAD, JUST A LITTLE *MOROSE* AT TIMES...

LOOK IT UP, I GOTTA GO.

BEEP

SORRY TO INTERRUPT YOUR EXPEDITION, ALLEN, BUT I JUST GOT A CALL YOU MIGHT BE INTERESTED IN...

I'M ALL EARS, DETECTIVE FARRUCI...

WE GOT A BURNED-OUT G.C.P.D. MOBILE TRANSPORTATION UNIT IN A PARKING GARAGE ON THE EDGE OF THE EAST END...

...LOOKS LIKE *SOMEBODY* WAS USING IT TO TRANSPORT *DRUGS.*

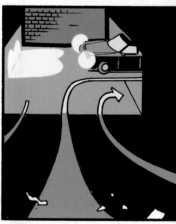

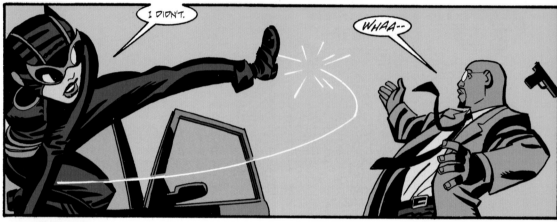

--LOOK, WE'VE GONE THROUGH IT TEN TIMES, SARGE, I DON'T KNOW WHAT MORE YOU WANT FROM ME...

I WANT SOMETHING TO MAKE *SENSE*, OKAY?

I WANT YOU TO EXPLAIN TO ME HOW *28 MILLION DOLLARS* IN DIAMONDS JUST *DISAPPEARS* FROM INSIDE A BRIEFCASE THAT'S HAND-CUFFED TO YOUR *DAMN* WRIST...

AND I *TOLD YOU*, I DON'T *KNOW*...

...THE VAN BLEW UP, I TURNED TO LOOK AT IT... AND NEXT THING I KNOW THE CASE IS OPEN AND EMPTY...

AND YOU DIDN'T SEE *ANYTHING?*

YEAH, I SAW A FEW HUNDRED KILOS OF HEROIN BURNING UP ALONG WITH THE WHOLE REST OF OUR LIVES... *THAT'S* WHAT I SAW.

YEAH, WELL... WE'LL JUST SEE ABOUT THAT, RICKETT...

AS LONG AS WE CAN RECOVER THOSE DIAMONDS IN THE NEXT DAY OR TWO, WE JUST MIGHT LIVE THROUGH THIS MESS...

HOW WE GONNA DO *THAT?*

I'M NOT SURE, BUT I'VE GOT A FEW IDEAS...

CAN'T BE TOO EASY TO MOVE THAT KINDA QUANTITY OF DIAMONDS... SO WE CAN START BY PUTTIN' THE SQUEEZE ON THE LOCAL FENCES...

NOW GRAB IVAN HERE'S LEGS AND LET'S GET RID OF SOME *EXCESS BAGGAGE...*

OH, GOOD, YOU'RE ALREADY UP...

ALREADY? HELL, I HARDLY SLEPT AT ALL LAST NIGHT, SISTER. THOUGHT I MIGHT AT LEAST CATCH A FEW HOURS, BUT I'M ANTSY...

I KNOW, BUT DON'T WORRY, WE'RE ALMOST THROUGH THIS... BY TONIGHT IT SHOULD ALL BE OVER.

EASY FOR YOU TO SAY, I'M THE ONE ABOUT TO BE HUNG OUT AS BAIT...

C'MON, SLAM... IF YOU THINK I'M GOING TO LET ANYTHING HAPPEN TO YOU, THEN YOU DON'T KNOW ME VERY WELL...

JUST REMEMBER I CAN'T DODGE BULLETS.

SO, WHAT HAPPENS NOW?

NOW I MAKE AN UNTRACEABLE PHONE CALL, AND IF THIS THING WORKS HOW IT SHOULD--

--I'LL SOUND LIKE A REAL TOUGH GUY...

YOU CARE TO TELL ME WHERE YOU PICKED UP A BRAND-NEW CELL PHONE?

OH, THESE THINGS ARE EVERYWHERE THESE DAYS--ACTUALLY I PICKED UP TWO OF THEM-- IT WAS THE VOICE MODIFIER THAT WAS HARD TO FIND...

SHHH-- IT'S RINGING.

Bleettleetlee

DAMN IT, CARMEN, I TOLD YOU AFTER THE NIGHT I'VE HAD TO HOLD ALL CALLS--

Bleettleettlee

Bleetleetleet

HELLO...?

SUPPOSE SOMEONE HAD 28 MILLION IN GEMS THAT BELONGED TO *YOU*, MISTER DYLAN--

--HOW MUCH, EXACTLY, WOULD YOU WANT THEM BACK?

WHO *IS* THIS?

THAT'S NOT IMPORTANT.

FOR NOW, I'M JUST THE GUY WHO HELPED STEAL YOUR DIAMONDS. THAT SHOULD BE ENOUGH.

Uh huh.... AND WHY ARE YOU OFFERING *ME* THIS DEAL, EXACTLY?

I WAS PAID TO DO A JOB--

--BUT I FIGURE THERE'S NO HARM IN TRYING TO GET A BETTER BID, RIGHT?

AND *WHO* PAID YOU, EXACTLY?

IF YOU'LL LOOK AT THE PHOTO IN THE ENVELOPE ON YOUR NIGHT TABLE--

--YOU'LL SEE ONE OF YOUR PLAYERS HAS SWITCHED SIDES.

THE MAN IN THE PHOTO IS SLAM BRADLEY, A LOW-LEVEL BAG-MAN FOR JUNIOR GALANTE...

...AS YOU CAN *SEE*, HE'S GETTING A HAND-OFF FROM OFFICER RICKETT.

I GUESS RICKETT WAS LOOKING FOR A BIGGER PAYCHECK...

WHICH EXPLAINS *HOW* YOU WERE ABLE TO EMPTY THE CASE WHILE IT WAS STILL ON HIS WRIST.

RIGHT... I'M *GOOD*, BUT I'M NOT *THAT* GOOD.

HE OPENED IT FOR ME WHILE EVERYONE WAS DISTRACTED AND THEN I GOT THE HELL OUT OF DODGE.

DID HE NOW?

LISTEN, WHY DON'T YOU MULL THIS OVER AND I'LL CALL YOU BACK ON THIS SAME LINE TONIGHT?

YES, I SHOULD HAVE A FIGURE FOR YOU BY THEN.

OH, AND MISTER DYLAN?

YES?

THAT'S *QUITE* AN APARTMENT YOU'VE GOT.

SORRY, I GOTTA TAKE THIS...

MORNIN', SIR. I DIDN'T THINK I'D BE HEARING FROM YOU THIS SOON. I THOUGHT WE'D HAVE A FEW DAYS TO--

YOU'RE KIDDING, RIGHT?

WELL, IT'S GOTTA BE SOME KINDA SCAM OR SOMETHING...

WHO? SLAM BRADLEY?

NO, THAT'S BUNK... I KNOW WHO THAT GUY IS, HE'S JUST A SHAMUS... HE DON'T--

OKAY, ALL RIGHT... LET ME LOOK INTO IT AND I'LL CALL YOU BACK.

HOLD ON, LEMME CHECK...

HEY, LOUIE, YOU GOT A FAX MACHINE I CAN USE?

UH... SURE, MacNALTY... IT'S IN THE BACK...

OKAY, LET ME MAKE ONE CALL AND I'LL GET RIGHT BACK TO YOU, YOU CAN SEND ME THE PHOTO HERE...

GOTHAM CENTRAL-- ORGANIZED CRIME...

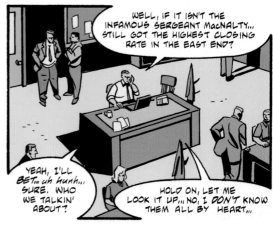

WELL, IF IT ISN'T THE INFAMOUS SERGEANT MacNALTY... STILL GOT THE HIGHEST CLOSING RATE IN THE EAST END?

YEAH, I'LL BET... uh hunh... SURE. WHO WE TALKIN' ABOUT?

HOLD ON, LET ME LOOK IT UP... NO, I DON'T KNOW THEM ALL BY HEART...

OKAY, HERE WE GO... BRADLEY...

YEP, HE'S SIGNED UP WITH THE BIG LEAGUES... JUST HAPPENED A FEW MONTHS AGO. WHY? HE A SUSPECT IN SOMETHING?

OH, A SNITCH MENTIONED HIM, huh?

WELL, GIVE US A CALL IF IT TURNS INTO ANYTHING, OKAY?

WELL, IT LOOKS LIKE I MADE A MISTAKE, LOUIE, SORRY ABOUT THE MESS...

I TOLD YOU I WAS CLEAN, MacNALTY... I WOULDN'T CROSS YOU.

I'M GONNA HAVE TO USE THAT FAX NOW...

ALLEN? YEAH, HE MADE THE CALL, JUST LIKE YOU THOUGHT... YEAH, I'M PRETTY SURE HE BOUGHT IT...

YEAH, WELL, I HOPE THIS SLAM BRADLEY GUY KNOWS WHAT HE'S DOING...

YOU NO-GOOD PIECE OF--

AHH!

KRAK

I SWEAR, SARGE... I DIDN'T DO NOTHIN'...

Y'KNOW, RICKETT, I BEEN THINKIN' ABOUT THIS ALL DAY... TRYIN' TO MAKE SENSE OF IT...

...AND THE SAD FACT IS, YOU'VE JUST ALWAYS BEEN TOO DAMN AMBITIOUS FOR YOUR OWN GOOD.

WHUU--

I-- huff huff-- I DIDN'T DO NOTHIN'... DUNNO --huff-- WHAT YOU'RE TALKIN' ABOUT...

THIS IS WHAT I'M TALKIN' ABOUT... YOU PASSING INFO TO A BAGMAN FOR THE MAFIA.

WHAT?

THAT GUY? HE WAS JUST SOME P.I. TRYING TO UNCOVER LEADS ON THAT CHICK WE TAGGED THE OTHER NIGHT...

HAD SOME PICTURES OF A FEW DIFFERENT GIRLS THAT HE THOUGHT MIGHT BE THEM...

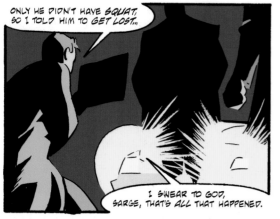

ONLY HE DIDN'T HAVE SQUAT, SO I TOLD HIM TO GET LOST...

I SWEAR TO GOD, SARGE, THAT'S ALL THAT HAPPENED.

Y'KNOW WHAT, BOYS? I THINK SOMEONE'S TRYING TO PULL A SCAM ON US.

SO MAYBE WE BETTER PAY THIS SHYLOCK A VISIT...

OKAY, SLAM, THEY'RE ON THEIR WAY UP... YOU READY?

AS MUCH AS I'LL EVER BE... YOU KNOW, SOMEDAY I'LL SHOW YOU THE PROPER WAY TO GO ABOUT GATHERING EVIDENCE.

...AS OPPOSED TO JUST MANUFACTURING IT.

ARE YOU SURE THEY AREN'T GONNA NOTICE THIS CAMERA?

TRUST ME, THIS IS STATE-OF-THE-ART, AND I DOUBT THEY'RE GONNA BE LOOKING TOO CLOSELY...

...AT LEAST NOT IF YOU PLAY YOUR PART RIGHT.

SLAM BRADLEY?

I THINK YOU KNOW WHO WE ARE... WE NEED TO TALK TO YOU.

SURE, FELLAS, COME ON IN... WHAT CAN I DO FOR YOU?

FOR STARTERS, YOU CAN TELL ME EXACTLY WHAT'S HAPPENING IN THIS PICTURE...

UH, WELL, I WAS SHOWING THE DETECTIVE A FEW PICTURES... TRYING TO PICK UP THE REWARD ON THAT GIRL THAT'S ON THE NEWS...

SEE, JUST LIKE I TOLD YOU.

OKAY, THEN, BRADLEY...

...SO WHAT'S A BAG MAN FOR JUNIOR GALANTE SO INTERESTED IN THIS GIRL FOR?

A BAG MAN? I THINK SOMEONE'S BEEN YANKIN' YOUR CHAIN... I'M JUST A P.I. TRYING TO TURN A FEW BUCKS...

SO, I'M GONNA ASK YOU THIS ONE TIME NICELY...

I WISH THAT WAS TRUE, BUT I TALKED TO O.C.B. THIS MORNIN'; NO DOUBT ABOUT IT, YOU'RE ON THE GALANTE PAYROLL...

BRADLEY INVESTIGATIONS

YOUR MAN BRADLEY'S GOT A LOT OF BALLS TO BE TRYIN' TO CON THESE GUYS... YOU THINK HE CAN HANDLE IT?

YEAH, I JUST HOPE HE DOESN'T ACT LIKE TOO MUCH OF A SMART-ASS...

...WHERE THE HELL ARE THE DIAMONDS?

WHAT IS THIS, OLD MOVIE NIGHT?

WHAKK!

ANSWER THE QUESTION, WISEGUY!

Y'KNOW, I COULD KILL YOU *RIGHT HERE*, AND NO ONE WOULD EVEN CARE...

IS THAT HOW IT WENT WITH THE GIRL?

UNTIL SHE GOT AWAY FROM YOU?

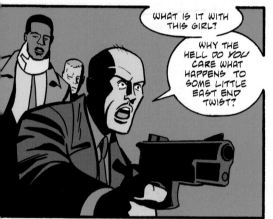

WHAT IS IT WITH THIS GIRL?

WHY THE HELL DO *YOU* CARE WHAT HAPPENS TO SOME LITTLE EAST END TWIST?

MY *EMPLOYER* IS INTERESTED IN WHAT SHE SAW THE NIGHT YOUR MEN SHOT HER...

SAYS IT'S GOOD TO KNOW WHEN COPS KILL OTHER COPS.

WHAT?! WHY WOULD THE *MAFIA* GIVE A DAMN IF WE TOOK OUT SOME UNDERCOVER SNITCH?

IS THIS SOME NEW TURF WAR?

TALK, BRADLEY... NOW OR NEVER AGAIN...

THIS IS GOING TOO FAR... I'M HEADING IN...

OKAY, JUST BACK UP OFFA ME A LITTLE AND I'LL TELL YOU EVERYTHING...

...YOU WITH ME OR--

SORRY ABOUT THIS, RICKETT, BUT IT'S YOU OR ME...

DROP IT, RICKETT, THERE'S NO WAY OUT OF THIS...

MAYBE NOT, BUT IT'S WORTH A SHOT...

...FIGURE I CAN TAKE *ONE* OF YOU WITH ME, FOR SURE...

FORGET IT. YOU *AREN'T* LEAVING THIS ROOM, UNLESS IT'S TO SEE HOW HIGH YOU BOUNCE.

THOUGHT YOU COULD HANG ME OUT TO DRY...YOU AND THIS OLD TURD...

WELL, GUESS AGAIN, GEEZER...

NOW GET THE HELL OUTTA MY WAY OR DIE!

DID YOU SAY... GEEZER?

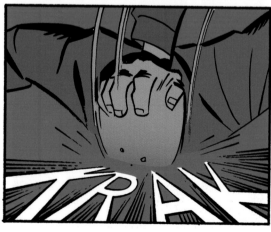

TRAK

GOOD TO SEE THIS OLD VEST STILL WORKS...

WHY DIDN'T YOU TELL ME ABOUT THAT THING?

HEY, I DIDN'T WANT YOU TO THINK I DIDN'T HAVE *FAITH* IN YOUR PLAN...

...SUCH AS IT WAS...

THERE WAS A *PLAN* BEHIND THIS DISASTER?

HARD TO BELIEVE...

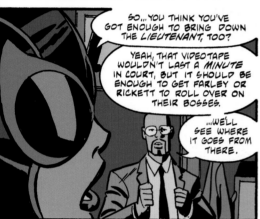

SO...YOU THINK YOU'VE GOT ENOUGH TO BRING DOWN THE *LIEUTENANT,* TOO?

YEAH, THAT VIDEOTAPE WOULDN'T LAST A *MINUTE* IN COURT, BUT IT SHOULD BE ENOUGH TO GET FARLEY OR RICKETT TO ROLL OVER ON THEIR BOSSES.

...WE'LL SEE WHERE IT GOES FROM THERE.

ABOUT THAT *TAPE...*

DON'T WORRY...IF YOU THINK I'M TURNING IN ANY VIDEO WITH YOU RUNNING AROUND IN THAT OUTFIT, YOU'RE CRAZIER THAN YOU LOOK.

I'LL JUST ERASE THAT PART AND SAY THE CAMERA GOT SHOT OR SOMETHING.

GOOD, NOW I BETTER GET OUT OF HERE BEFORE THE REST OF THE CITY'S COPS SHOW UP.

MAN, SHE'S REALLY *SOMETHING,* ISN'T SHE?

BROTHER, YOU SAID A MOUTH- FUL...

ALL RIGHT, NOW LET'S GET OUR STORY STRAIGHT, BRADLEY...

SO WHAT'S IT GOING TO BE, MATTHEWS? YOU GIVE US YOUR BOSSES, AND WE MAY BE ABLE TO SWING *20 YEARS,* OTHERWISE YOU'RE LOOKING AT *LIFE.*

AT LEAST WITH LIFE IN PRISON, I'LL BE ALIVE.

JUST SAY NO!

PERSONALLY, I WISH THEY GAVE THE DEATH PENALTY TO DIRTY COPS.

FROM WHAT I HEAR, THAT'S JUST WHAT YOU DID TO SERGEANT MacNALTY TONIGHT.

IS THAT SUPPOSED TO MAKE ME FEEL BAD? 'CAUSE IT DOESN'T.

YOU WANT TO SPEND THE REST OF YOUR LIFE IN A BOX, THAT'S YOUR CHOICE...

OKAY, LOOK. WHAT IF THERE WAS *SOMETHING ELSE* I COULD GIVE YOU?

WHAT?

A BOOK. LIKE A LEDGER, WITH THE NAMES OF ALL THE COPS THAT'RE ON THE TAKE... WOULD *THAT* HELP ME AT ALL?

IT MIGHT.

OKAY, IN THE BASE-MENT OF MY HOUSE, THERE'S A BUNCH OF PIPES RUNNING ALONG THE CEILING...

...WHERE THEY MEET THE WALL, THERE'S A BRICK THAT MOVES...

THERE'S *NO WAY* ANY OF YOUR SEARCH TEAM'VE FOUND IT...

--UNFORTUNATELY, POLICE WERE UNABLE TO LOCATE A NOTEBOOK ALLEGEDLY KEPT BY LIEUTENANT MATTHEWS WHICH HELD A RECORD OF ALL THE CORRUPT COPS IN HIS PRECINCT...

AT THIS POINT, WE'RE UNCERTAIN THAT ANY SUCH NOTEBOOK *EVER* ACTUALLY EXISTED OR IF LIEUTENANT MATTHEWS WAS JUST TRYING TO LEAD US ASTRAY...

NOTEBOOK, *huh?* YOU KNOW ANYTHING ABOUT THAT?

YEAH, I DO...

"THEY WON'T BE FINDING IT."

We're even

CREESUS, SELINA, THAT BOOK COULDA TIED THE *KNOT* ON THIS *WHOLE CASE...* WHAT'D YOU *DO?*

I MADE A DEAL TO GET THE INFORMATION ABOUT THAT DRUG DROP, AND I *KEEP* MY *WORD.*

YEAH, BUT--

THERE IS NO *BUT,* SLAM. THIS WHOLE THING WAS ALL ABOUT SAVING *HOLLY...* THAT'S *ALL* I CARED ABOUT.

ANY COP THAT BOOK BROUGHT DOWN--

--WOULD JUST BE REPLACED BY TWO MORE THE NEXT DAY, ANYWAY, SO WHAT'S THE DIFFERENCE?

IN RELATED NEWS, AUTHORITIES ARE *NO LONGER* LOOKING FOR THE UNKNOWN GIRL PREVIOUSLY SOUGHT IN CONNECTION WITH THE DEATH OF A G.C.P.D. *UNDERCOVER* OFFICER...

DETECTIVE ALLEN HAD THIS TO SAY...

...AS OF RIGHT NOW, WE'RE FAIRLY CERTAIN THAT GIRL WAS A FABRICATION BY SERGEANT MacNALTY, AS PART OF HIS ATTEMPTED COVER-UP...

SO, WHERE IS THE SQUIRT, ANYWAY?

"OH... SHE FELT OKAY TO WALK...

"SO SHE WENT TO VISIT A FRIEND... "

HEY, KARON... HOW'S IT GOIN'?

OH MY GOD... YOU ARE IN SO MUCH TROUBLE...

DO YOU HAVE ANY IDEA WHAT YOU PUT ME THROUGH THE LAST FEW DAYS?

I KNOW, I'M SORRY... IF YOU WANT, THOUGH, I'LL SHOW YOU MY BULLET WOUND...

I'VE GOT A BETTER IDEA... HOW ABOUT WE JUST CURL UP ON MY COUCH AND WATCH SOME TV?

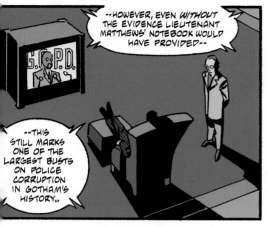

--HOWEVER, EVEN *WITHOUT* THE EVIDENCE LIEUTENANT MATTHEWS' NOTEBOOK WOULD HAVE PROVIDED--

--THIS STILL MARKS ONE OF THE LARGEST BUSTS ON POLICE CORRUPTION IN GOTHAM'S HISTORY...

THE LAST FEW DAYS *HAVE* PUT A MAJOR KINK IN OUR PLANS, MISTER DYLAN.

I KNOW, SIR.

I DIDN'T SPEND ALL THIS TIME CARVING OUT A PIECE OF THE EAST END TO JUST LET IT GO TO WASTE.

IT *HAD* TO BE *CATWOMAN,* SIR, NO ONE ELSE COULD HAVE PULLED OFF SUCH AN ELABORATE SCAM...

YOU DON'T NEED TO CONVINCE ME... I'VE BEEN *WONDERING* WHAT SHE WAS UP TO--

--EVER SINCE SHE CONVINCED THAT *DEALER* TO TURN ON YOU...

...BUT NOW I *SEE* THAT SHE'S MORE OF A *PROBLEM* THAN WE EVER ANTICIPATED...

SO I THINK IT'S JUST ABOUT TIME FOR HER TO LEARN WHAT HAPPENS WHEN YOU CROSS THE *BLACK MASK.*

THE END FOR NOW....

CATWOMAN GOES STRAIGHT
BATMAN #62

When Catwoman was first introduced in *Batman* #1 (June 1940), the tradition of the femme fatale was strong in all forms of crime fiction, and it seemed Batman had acquired an adversary for life. However, throughout the 1940s public opinion changed towards the darker aspects of comics, leading to a code of practice being agreed in 1948. Just two years later, Bill Finger wrote 'The Secret Life of the Catwoman,' revealing she was not so bad after all. It had taken 10 years for her origin to be revealed and for Catwoman to be named Selina Kyle.

Catwoman next appeared in *Batman* #65 (June 1951) in the story 'Catwoman, Empress of the Underworld'. A sudden streak of cat-themed crimes suggested that Selina had gone back on her word. In fact, the crimes were committed by a mobster trying to force Catwoman's hand and lure her back into her bad old ways. She remained an ally of Batman for this issue.

Readers were once again teased with the possibility that Catwoman had turned evil in *Batman* #69 (Feb 1952) in 'The King of the Cats'. In this case, her sudden fraternising with a new, male, cat-themed super villain was explained by the fact that he was her brother and she had set her mind on persuading him to give up his nefarious career.

Selina finally returned to a life of crime in *Detective Comics* #203 (Jan 1954). The cover emphasised her return to the dark side by showing her threatening the Dynamic Duo with a cat o' nine tails. She continued her criminal ways in *Detective Comics* #211 (Sep 1954), after which pressure from the newly formed Comics Code led to a thirteen-year absence for Selina.

Which side is she on? A life of crime proved difficult for Catwoman to resist.

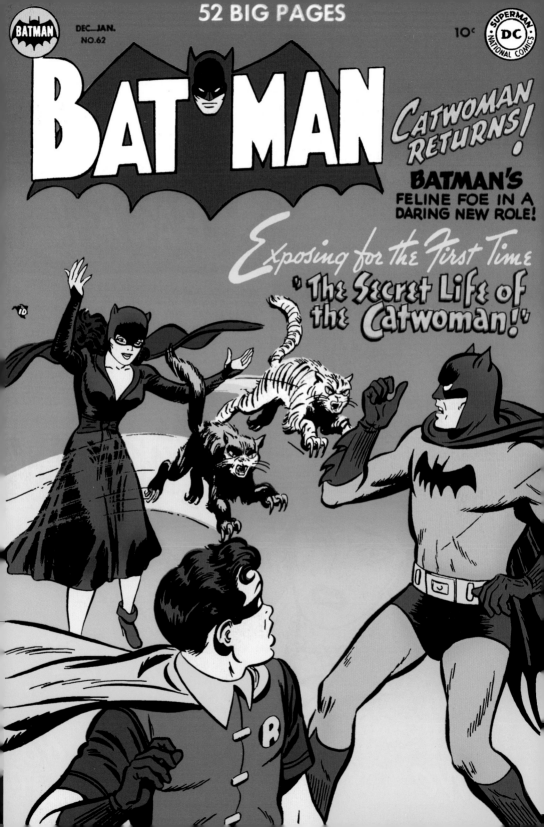

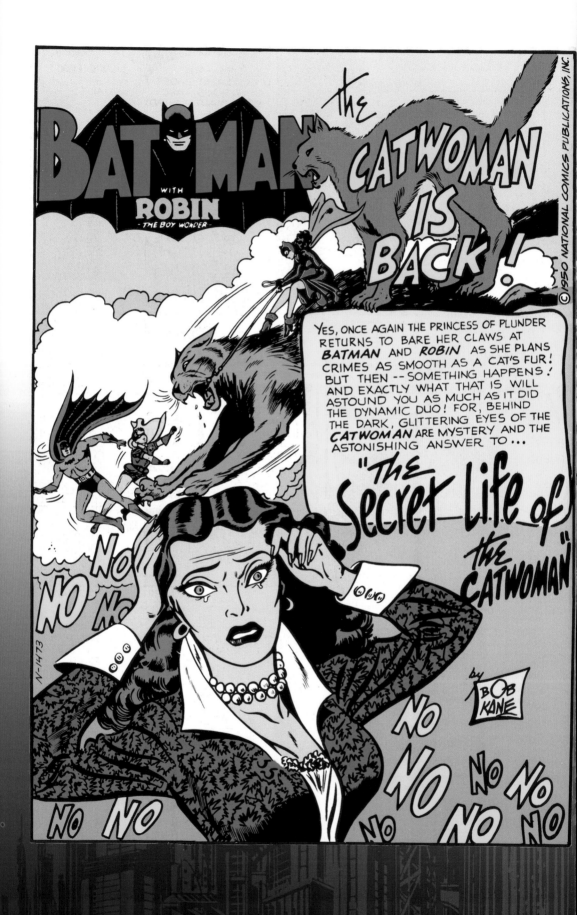

CATWOMAN, YOU ALWAYS ROB WITHOUT KILLING, BY USING YOUR KNOWLEDGE OF CATS! SO HERE'S MY OFFER -- YOU DO THE JOBS FOR ME, AND WE'LL SHARE THE LOOT! IF YOU REFUSE, I'LL DO THE JOBS ANYWAY! WHAT DO YOU SAY?

OKAY -- WE'RE PARTNERS!

GOOD! DIPPER, HERE, WILL TELL YOU OF THE FIRST PLACE TO BE ROBBED! BY THE TIME WE'RE THROUGH, WE'LL HAVE COMMISSIONER GORDON GOING AROUND IN CIRCLES!

LATER, AS THE CATWOMAN AND DIPPER DISCUSS ROBBERY PLANS IN A CRIMINAL HANGOUT...

HYA, DIPPER OL' PAL! DID-DIDJA TALK TO MISTER X ABOUT ME JOINING HIS MOB, HUH?

BEAT IT, MOUSEY! MISTER X DON'T WANT YOU AROUND! HE LIKES GUYS WITH NERVE! IF THE COPS EVER LOOKED AT YOU, YOU'D FAINT.

AW, PLEASE, DIPPER. I'LL DO ANYTHING TO JOIN THE MOB! UGH! DON'T SHOVE!

HE'S ALWAYS AROUND, CATWOMAN! A REGULAR PEST! HE'S JUST LIKE HIS NAME -- MOUSEY!

CAREFUL MOUSEY, OR I'LL SEND THIS CAT AFTER YOU! HA-HA!

SPLAT

MEOWRR

LATER, IN THE CATWOMAN'S EERIE LAIR...

YAWN! I HATE TO LEAVE THIS WARM FIRE AND MY PRETTY PETS-- BUT IT'S TIME I LOOKED OVER THE FIRST PLACE I'M TO ROB! YAWN

MEOWRRR

PURR-RR

PURR-RR

BUT AS SHE STEPS OUT INTO THE NIGHT...

YOUR HUNCH WAS RIGHT, BATMAN! HER HIDEOUT IS SOMEWHERE AROUND HERE! LET'S GO!

LOOK, ROBIN! IT'S THE CATWOMAN!

LATER, WHEN SELINA KYLE EXPLAINS THE FACTS TO THE COMMISSIONER...

CATWOMAN... ER... I MEAN MISS KYLE, IF YOU WISH TO ATONE FOR YOUR PAST CRIMES, YOU CAN DO SO BY BECOMING OUR **UNDERCOVER AGENT!**

THAT'S RIGHT, SELINA... YOU'RE OUR BEST LEAD TO **MISTER X**, SO WE WANT YOU TO **REMAIN AS HIS PARTNER!**

NO... PLEASE! I WANT TO PUT MY CRIMINAL PAST BEHIND ME!

YOU **WILL**... BUT AFTERWARD! REMEMBER, IF YOU PRETEND TO BE **MISTER X'S** PARTNER, THERE'LL BE **NO MORE KILLINGS!** YOU'LL BE DOING A PUBLIC SERVICE! AND IF MY PLAN WORKS, YOU'LL ONLY HAVE TO DO **ONE JOB!**

WITH YOU AS OUR SECRET OPERATIVE, WE'LL GET **MISTER X**, AND... WHA..?

COMMISSIONER, I JUST PICKED UP THIS PUNK FOR CARRYING A GUN! HE... ULP! SORRY, SIR... I THOUGHT YOU WERE ALONE!

MOUSEY!

THIS MAN IS DANGEROUS! HE'S ALWAYS WANTED TO JOIN **MR. X'S** GANG! NOW, HE'LL SURELY TELL **MR. X** ABOUT ME -- AS A BRIBE!

IN THAT CASE, WE MUST LOCK HIM UP! OFFICER, CHARGE HIM WITH CARRYING A CONCEALED WEAPON... NOBODY'S TO SEE HIM TILL THIS CASE IS FINISHED!

HUH? I'LL GET YOU FOR THIS, **CAT-WOMAN!**

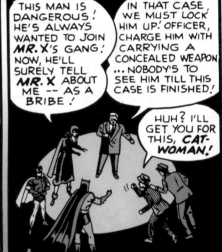

AFTER MOUSEY IS LED OFF...

WELL, SELINA KYLE... ALIAS THE **CATWOMAN**, YOU'RE NOW WORKING **FOR** THE LAW! DON'T FORGET THAT!

I WON'T -- UNLESS I GET **AMNESIA** AGAIN! I WAS SCARED, BUT NOT ANYMORE... NOT WHILE MOUSEY IS SAFELY LOCKED UP!

BUT IS HE? FOR AS SOON AS THE FURTIVE LITTLE CROOK IS ALONE IN HIS CELL...

HA, HA... LUCKY THOSE COPPERS DIDN'T FIND THIS FILE HIDDEN IN MY SHOE! ONCE I GET OUT, IT'LL BE BYE-BYE **CATWOMAN!**

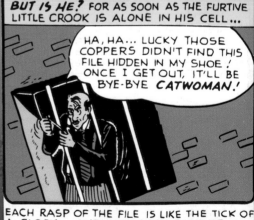

EACH RASP OF THE FILE IS LIKE THE TICK OF A CLOCK... AND WITH EACH PASSING MOMENT, DEATH LOOMS CLOSER FOR SELINA KYLE -- ALIAS THE **CATWOMAN!**

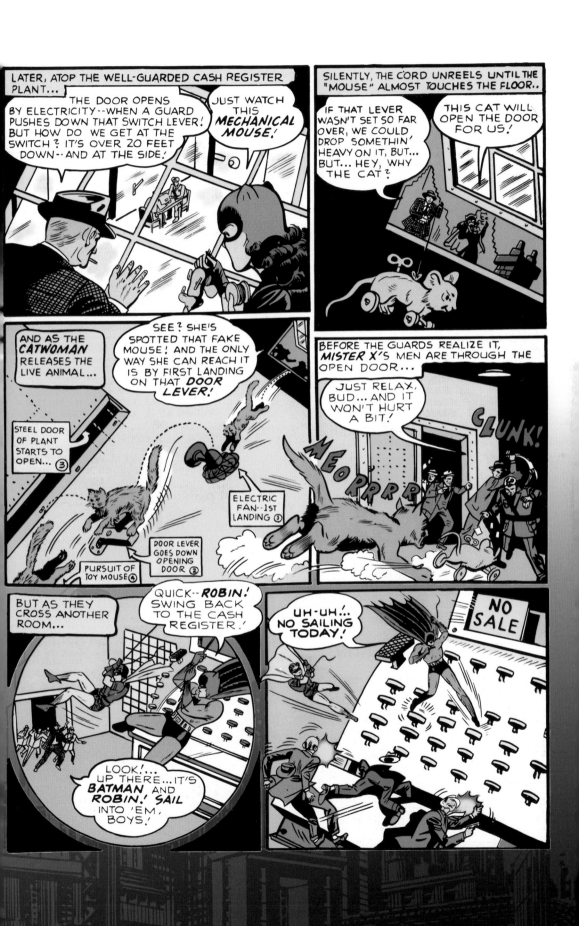

MISSED, *BLAST 'EM!* THEY KEEP HOPPING AROUND!

TIME FOR ME TO GO INTO ACTION!

MOMENTS LATER, A LENGTHENED *CAT-O'-NINE-TAILS* SNAPS OUT AT THE MASKED LAWMEN, AND...

HEY! *CATWOMAN* GOT 'EM FROM THE CATWALK! START SHOOTIN', BOYS!

NO! DON'T SHOOT! I WANT THEM *ALIVE!*

HUH? WHAT'S WHAT'S THE MATTER, *CATWOMAN?* GOIN' SOFT!

FOOLS! MY DEAL WITH *MISTER X* DIDN'T INCLUDE THE CAPTURE OF *BATMAN* AND *ROBIN!* I WANT A *BONUS* FOR THIS, AND I DON'T TALK *BUSINESS* TILL I SEE *MISTER X IN PERSON!*

OKAY! THIS IS IMPORTANT ENOUGH FOR ME TO CONTACT HIM!

YOUR PLAN'S WORKING, *BATMAN!* AT LAST, WE'RE GOING TO MEET *MISTER X!*

YES, *ROBIN*, BUT WE MUST REMAIN CAREFUL... LETTING OURSELVES BE "CAPTURED" IS ONLY HALF THE JOB! FROM NOW ON, ONE SLIPUP, AND WE'RE DEAD DUCKS!

AT THAT MOMENT, IN MOUSEY'S CELL...

AHH.. TWO BARS OUT--ONE TO GO! IT WON'T BE LONG NOW-- SOON, IT'S GONNA BE CURTAINS FOR THE *CATWOMAN!*

AND WILL IT ALSO BE CURTAINS FOR *BATMAN* AND *ROBIN?* FOR IF THE *CATWOMAN* DIES, THE PLAN TO RESCUE *BATMAN* AND *ROBIN* DIES WITH HER!

HOURS LATER, IN A DESERTED FARMHOUSE ON THE OUTSKIRTS OF GOTHAM CITY...

DIPPER EXPLAINED EVERYTHING, *CATWOMAN!* YOU DID A FINE JOB! BOYS, TAKE THEIR UTILITY BELTS AWAY--I'VE GOT PLANS FOR *BATMAN* AND *ROBIN!*

AND WE'VE GOT PLANS FOR YOU, TOO, *MISTER X!*

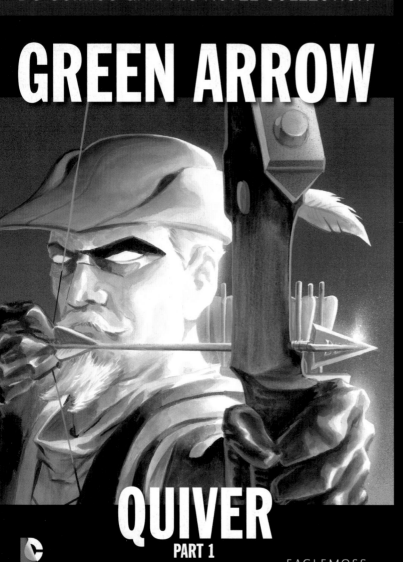

VOLUME 38

Many questions surround the resurrected Green Arrow. And now,
supernatural entities are closing in to bring his new life to a quick end.

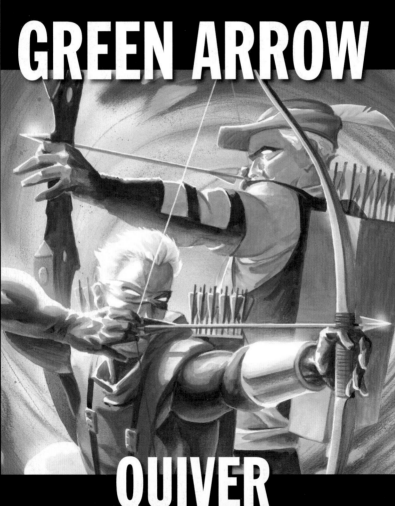

DC COMICS GRAPHIC NOVEL COLLECTION

GREEN ARROW

QUIVER
PART 2

DC COMICS

EAGLEMOSS
COLLECTIONS

PLUS BLACK CANARY'S FIRST APPEARANCES FROM *FLASH COMICS* #86 & 92

GRANT MORRISON

BATMAN & ROBIN VOL. 1: BATMAN REBORN with FRANK QUITELY & PHILIP TAN

VOL. 2: BATMAN VS. ROBIN

VOL. 3: BATMAN & ROBIN MUST DIE!

DARK KNIGHT VS. WHITE KNIGHT

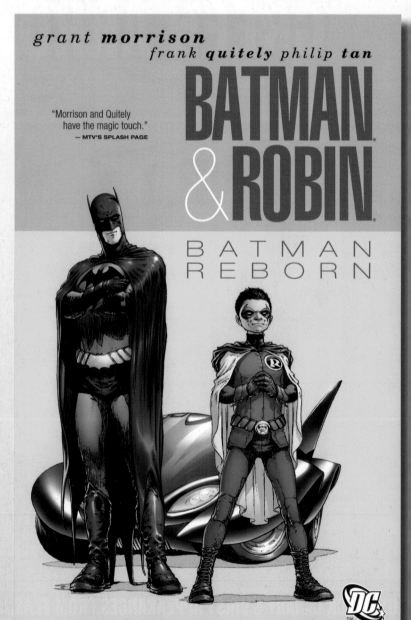